Special Edition to Support the works of

Minhaj Welfare Foundation
298 Romford Road, London, E7 9HD

UK: 0300 30 30 777
EU: +44 (0) 203 375 4730
USA/Canada: 1-888-9-MINHAJ [646425]

www.minhajwelfare.org

Zakah & Charity

ESSENTIAL QUESTIONS AND EXPLANATIONS

Compiled from the works of
SHAYKH-UL-ISLAM DR
MUHAMMAD TAHIR-UL-QADRI

Minhaj-ul-Quran Publications

ZAKAH & CHARITY

ESSENTIAL QUESTIONS AND EXPLANATIONS

COMPILED FROM THE WORKS OF

SHAYKH-UL-ISLAM DR
MUHAMMAD TAHIR-UL-QADRI

Translated by
Jawed Iqbal Tahiri

Compiled and Edited by
Shaykh Sohail Ahmad Siddiqui, Farida Sajjad, Misbah Kabeer and Waqas Ahmed Amin

MINHAJ-UL-QURAN PUBLICATIONS

Author: Dr Muhammad Tahir-ul-Qadri

Published by
Minhaj-ul-Quran Publications
292–296 Romford Road
Forest Gate, E7 9HD
London (UK)

All proceeds from the books, literature and audio-visual media (all multimedia) delivered by Dr Muhammad Tahir-ul-Qadri are entirely donated to Minhaj-ul-Quran International (MQI).

Translation and Editorial Team
Jawed Iqbal Tahiri, Shaykh Sohail Ahmad Siddiqui and Waqas Ahmed Amin

A catalogue record for this book is available from the British Library.

ISBN: 978-1-908229-25-0
www.minhaj.org | www.minhajuk.org
www.minhajpublications.com

First published May 2014

Printed by Mega Printing, Turkey

Transliteration Key

ا/ آ/ ى	ā	ظ	ẓ
ب	b	ع	ʿ
ت	t	غ	gh
ث	th	ف	f
ج	j	ق	q
ح	ḥ	ك	k
خ	kh	ل	l
د	d	م	m
ذ	dh	ن	n
ر	r	ه	h
ز	z	و	w/ū
س	s	ي	y/ī
ش	sh	ة	a
ص	ṣ	ء	ʾ
ض	ḍ	أ	a
ط	ṭ	إ	i

Contents

Q.1. What is zakah?

A: Zakah is one of the fundamental pillars of Islam which is also known as *al-ṣadaqa al-wājiba* (obligatory almsgiving). According to the Shariah, someone who qualifies for the *niṣāb* must spend a specific amount of his or her wealth upon those who are eligible to receive Zakah so that their poverty is alleviated.

Q.2. What are the linguistic and legal meanings of zakah?

A: Linguistically speaking, the word zakah bears two meanings: the first meaning is purity, and the second is growth.[1]

The first meaning of zakah, which means purity, can be understood from the following verses of the Qurʾān:

﴿قَدْ أَفْلَحَ مَن زَكَّىٰهَا ۝٩ وَقَدْ خَابَ مَن دَسَّىٰهَا﴾

> *Indeed, the one who purifies his (ill-commanding) self (from all vain and vicious desires and cultivate in its virtues and piousness) succeeds, but the one who corrupts himself (in sins and suppresses virtue) is doomed indeed.*[2]

The concept of success which is given by these verses through the purification of the inner-self, gives zakah the meaning of purifying wealth from all impurities by spending in the way of Allah.

---

[1] Ibn Manẓūr, *Lisān al-ʿArab*, 14:358.
[2] Qurʾān 91:9-10.

The second meaning of zakah is growth. For example, a field which yields crops is said in Arabic:

زَكَا الزَّرْعُ.

The crops grew.

Keeping this meaning in mind, zakah refers to wealth which does not decrease when spent in the path of Allah, but grows by Allah's blessing. The Qurʾān states:

﴿وَيُرْبِي ٱلصَّدَقَٰتِ﴾

> *...and multiplies alms gifts (i.e., increasing blessings of clean wealth manifold through charity donation)...*[1]

It is narrated from Abū Hurayra that the Holy Prophet ﷺ said:

مَا نَقَصَتْ صَدَقَةٌ مِنْ مَالٍ.

Charity does not reduce wealth.[2]

Q.3. WHEN WAS ZAKAH OBLIGATED?

A: *Ṣadaqa al-fiṭr* was obligated in the second year after *hijra* in the illuminated city of Medina, with the remaining rulings being obligated later during that year. Generally speaking, zakah was made obligatory during the Meccan period, similar to the way the ritual prayer was initiated in the beginning of Islam. However, the comprehensive system of zakah was completed after the Conquest of Mecca. In the early days, zakah was synonymous for charity and almsgiving. The amount to be paid and the condition of being over the *niṣāb* threshold

---

[1] Ibid., 2:276.
[2] Narrated by Muslim in *al-Ṣaḥīḥ*, 4:2001 §2588.

after the passing of a year, alongside other rulings that pertain to zakah, were enforced later on.

The message and call of the Holy Prophet ﷺ was that of *ḥuqūq Allāh* (the rights of Allah) and *ḥuqūq al-ʿibād* (the rights of people). The greatest manifestation of *ḥuqūq Allāh* is the ritual prayer and the most comprehensive representation of *ḥuqūq al-ʿibād* is zakah. Before the declaration of Prophethood, the Holy Prophet ﷺ used to worship Allah in solitude, and he also used to discretely see to the needs of the poor, needy, orphans and widows.

Sūra al-Muzammil is one of the early chapters to be revealed. In this chapter there is the commandment of zakah. Allah ﷻ says:

﴿وَأَقِيمُوا۟ ٱلصَّلَوٰةَ وَءَاتُوا۟ ٱلزَّكَوٰةَ وَأَقْرِضُوا۟ ٱللَّهَ قَرْضًا حَسَنًا ۚ وَمَا تُقَدِّمُوا۟ لِأَنفُسِكُم مِّنْ خَيْرٍ تَجِدُوهُ عِندَ ٱللَّهِ هُوَ خَيْرًا وَأَعْظَمَ أَجْرًا ۚ وَٱسْتَغْفِرُوا۟ ٱللَّهَ ۖ إِنَّ ٱللَّهَ غَفُورٌ رَّحِيمٌۢ﴾

And establish prayer and pay zakah (the alms-due) and lend Allah a goodly loan. And whatever good you will send forward for yourselves, you will find it in the presence of Allah much better and in reward still greater. And keep seeking forgiveness from Allah. Allah is Most Forgiving, Ever-Merciful.[1]

In the fifth year after the declaration of Prophethood, when Jaʿfar al-Ṭayyār and other Companions migrated to Abyssinia, they were summoned by the King (*Najjāshī*) and questioned about Islam and its teachings. Replying to his inquiry, Jaʿfar al-Ṭayyār said:

---

[1] Qurʾān 73:20.

أَمَرَنَا بِالصَّلٰوةِ وَالزَّكَاةِ وَالصِّيَامِ.

> He [the Holy Prophet ﷺ] has commanded us to perform the ritual prayer, pay the zakah and to fast.[1]

From this it is clear that zakah was initiated in the early years of Islam. In 6 AH, when Heraclius received the Holy Prophet's letter, he asked Abū Sufyān about the Prophet ﷺ and his teachings. Although Abū Sufyān had not yet accepted Islam, he was compelled to state:

يَأْمُرُنَا بِالصَّلٰوةِ وَالزَّكَاةِ وَالصِّلَةِ وَالْعَفَافِ.

> He commands us to perform the ritual prayer, pay the zakah, keep family ties, and to remain chaste.[2]

These events make it clear that the zakah, in its primal form, was initiated in the early days of Islam.

Q.4. Is it obligatory according to the Qur'ān and Sunna to pay the zakah?

A: According to the Qur'ān and Sunna, paying the zakah is obligatory (*farḍ*) for the one who holds wealth in excess of the *niṣāb*. Denying the obligation of the zakah is *kufr* (disbelief).

Allah ﷻ states in the Qur'ān:

﴿وَءَاتُواْ ٱلزَّكَوٰةَ﴾

> *And pay zakah (the alms-due).*[3]

---

[1] Narrated by Aḥmad b. Ḥanbal in *al-Musnad*, 1:202 and 5:291; and Ibn Khuzayma in *al-Ṣaḥīḥ*, 4:13 §2260.
[2] Narrated by al-Bukhārī in *al-Ṣaḥīḥ*, 2:505 and 4:1658 §4278; and Muslim in *al-Ṣaḥīḥ*, 3:1395 §1773.
[3] Qur'ān 2:83.

The repeated emphasis on a ruling is proof of its importance. In the Qurʾān, the command emphasising on the payment of zakah appears eighty-two (82) times. In the same way the command on paying the zakah is given in numerous hadiths.

1. ʿAbd Allāh b. ʿUmar narrates that the Prophet ﷺ said:

بُنِيَ الْإِسْلَامُ عَلَى خَمْسٍ: شَهَادَةِ أَنْ لَا إِلَهَ إِلَّا اللهُ وَأَنَّ مُحَمَّدًا رَسُولُ اللهِ، وَإِقَامِ الصَّلَاةِ، وَإِيتَاءِ الزَّكَاةِ، وَالْحَجِّ، وَصَوْمِ رَمَضَانَ.

Islam is built on five: testifying that there is no deity except Allah and that Muhammad is Allah's Messenger; the performing of the ritual prayer; paying zakah, the Pilgrimage; and the fast of *Ramaḍān*.[1]

2. Ḥasan al-Baṣrī narrates that the Prophet ﷺ said:

حَصِّنُوا أَمْوَالَكُمْ بِالزَّكَاةِ وَدَاوُوا أَمْرَاضَكُمْ بِالصَّدَقَةِ، وَاسْتَقْبِلُوا أَمْوَاجَ الْبَلَاءِ بِالدُّعَاءِ وَالتَّضَرُّعِ.

Secure your wealth through the payment of zakah; cure your illnesses through the donation of charity; and face the waves of difficulty through supplication and humility [before the presence of Allah].[2]

3. Abū Hurayra narrates that the Prophet ﷺ said:

إِذَا أَدَّيْتَ زَكَاةَ مَالِكَ فَقَدْ قَضَيْتَ مَا عَلَيْكَ.

---

[1] Narrated by al-Bukhārī in *al-Ṣaḥīḥ*, 1:12 §8; and Muslim in *al-Ṣaḥīḥ*, 1:45 §16.

[2] Narrated by Abū Dāwūd in *al-Sunan*, 1:62 §96; al-Ṭabarānī in *al-Muʿjam al-awsaṭ*, 2:274 §1963; and al-Bayhaqī in *Shuʿab al-īmān*, 3:285 §3557.

> When you have paid the zakah on your wealth, you have fulfilled your duty.[1]

4. When the Holy Prophet ﷺ appointed Muʿādh b. Jabal as the governor of Yemen, he gave him the following guidance:

> You are going to a people who are people of the book. So call them to bear witness that there is no deity but Allah, and that I am the Messenger of Allah. If they obey you in this respect, tell them that Allah has prescribed five prayers on them every day and night. If they obey you in this regard tell them that Allah has prescribed alms-due on their property and returned it to their poor. If they obey you in this respect, do not take the best of their property. Beware of the curse of the oppressed, for there is no curtain between it and Allah.[2]

Q.5. WHAT ARE THE CONDITIONS FOR THE OBLIGATION OF ZAKAH?

A: The following conditions must be fulfilled in order for zakah to be obligatory upon an individual:

1. Being a Muslim: zakah is not obligatory on non-Muslims.
2. Maturity: zakah is not obligatory upon children.
3. Sanity: zakah is not obligatory on those who are mentally handicapped.
4. Being free: zakah is not obligatory on prisoners.
5. To be in complete ownership of wealth: the wealth can only be subject to zakah if it is in complete ownership of the individual. For example, if someone buried his possessions somewhere and forgot where

---

[1] Narrated by al-Tirmidhī in *al-Jāmiʿ al-Ṣaḥīḥ*, 3:13 §618.
[2] Narrated by Abū Dāwūd in *al-Sunan*, 2:18 §1584.

he buried it, but years later he regained his lost possession, then he will not have to pay zakah during the interim period when the possession was missing.

6. The wealth should be surplus of one's basic necessities.
7. To be free of debt: if someone has £1000 in saving, but also has a debt to pay of £1000, that person is not free from debt thus he is not required to pay the zakah.
8. Zakah is payable on that wealth and property which grows, either tangibly such as trade stocks or grazing animals, or in value such as gold and silver.
9. The total value of the wealth and property must be above the payable threshold (*niṣāb*) as determined by the Shariah.
10. The person must be in possession of that wealth, which is above the *niṣāb* value, for a complete lunar year. That is, zakah does not become obligatory simply by possessing wealth in excess of the *niṣāb*, one must also be above the *niṣāb* value after a whole lunar year has passed.

Q.6. Is an intention required when paying zakah?

A: Yes, in order to fulfil the obligation of zakah the intention (*niyya*) is required, as it is an act of worship. The intention (*niyya*) for performing the zakah is to make a firm resolve that the wealth one is giving away or putting aside is for the purpose of paying the zakah.

Q.7. What is the wisdom behind obligating the zakah?

A: As zakah is related to money and finance, it plays a central role in Islamic economics. The wisdoms behind the obligation of zakah are many, some of which are mentioned below:

1. Wealth is purified and blessed.
2. The poor and needy of society are given financial support.
3. One receives protection from the miserliness and greed of the lower self (*nafs*).
4. On receiving the blessing of wealth, a desire stems from the heart to show gratitude to Allah ﷻ.

It is the duty of the Islamic state, through the means of zakah, to provide an economic system and social structure by which all illicit (*ḥarām*) means of income are put to an end and the doors to lawful (*ḥalāl*) income are opened. In this way not only will the means of earning a living for all individuals be lawful, but the vices which are found in society will be also eradicated. Furthermore, the society as a whole will be familiar with the boundaries set by the Shariah thus making it prosper in the long run.

Q.8. WHAT ARE THE VIRTUES OF PAYING ZAKAH?

A: Being a very important pillar of Islam, a great amount has been mentioned regarding the virtue of paying zakah. In light of the hadiths, the person who discharges his obligation of zakah will not only go to Paradise, rather Paradise will be guaranteed for him.

1. ʿUmayr al-Laythī narrates that the Prophet ﷺ said during his Farewell sermon:

إِنَّ أَوْلِيَاءَ اللهِ الْـمُصَلُّونَ، وَمَنْ يُقِيمُ الصَّلَوَاتِ الْخَمْسَ الَّتِي
كَتَبَهُنَّ اللهُ عَلَيْهِ، وَيَصُومُ رَمَضَانَ وَيَحْتَسِبُ صَوْمَهُ، وَيُؤْتِي الزَّكَاةَ
مُحْتَسِبًا طَيِّبَةً بِهَا نَفْسُهُ، وَيَجْتَنِبُ الْكَبَائِرَ الَّتِي نَهَى اللهُ عَنْهَا.

The friends of Allah are those who perform the ritual prayers; and whoever establishes the five ritual prayers which Allah has prescribed upon people, fasts in the month of *Ramaḍān* hoping for reward, gives zakah readily and refrains from the major sins which Allah has prohibited.[1]

2. Abū Hurayra relates that the Holy Prophet ﷺ said to the people sitting around him: 'If you give me a guarantee of six things, I will guarantee Paradise for you.' Abū Hurayra asked, 'O Messenger of Allah, what are those (six things)?' The Holy Prophet ﷺ said:

الصَّلَاةُ وَالزَّكَاةُ وَالْأَمَانَةُ وَالْفَرْجُ وَالْبَطْنُ وَاللِّسَانِ.

They are the ritual prayer, the zakah, trust, the private parts, the stomach and the tongue.[2]

3. The one who fulfils the obligation of zakah each year tastes the flavour of *īmān* (faith). It is narrated by ʿAbd Allāh b. Muʿāwiya al-Ghāḍirī that the Holy Prophet ﷺ said:

ثَلَاثٌ مَنْ فَعَلَهُنَّ فَقَدْ طَعِمَ طَعْمَ الْإِيمَانِ: مَنْ عَبَدَ اللهَ وَحْدَهُ وَأَنَّهُ لَا إِلَهَ إِلَّا اللهُ وَأَعْطَى زَكَاةَ مَالِهِ طَيِّبَةً بِهَا نَفْسُهُ رَافِدَةً عَلَيْهِ كُلَّ عَامٍ.

Whoever performs three things he will taste the flavour of faith (*īmān*): whoever worships Allah alone that there is no deity except Allah; pays zakah each year willingly and happily...[3]

4. Muʿādh b. Jabal narrates that the Holy Prophet ﷺ said:

---

[1] Narrated by al-Ṭabarānī in *al-Muʿjam al-kabīr*, 17:47 §101; al-Ḥākim in *al-Mustadrak*, 1:127 §197; and al-Bayhaqī in *al-Sunan al-kubrā*, 10:186 §20,541.

[2] Narrated by al-Ṭabarānī in *al-Muʿjam al-awsaṭ*, 5:154 §4925.

[3] Narrated by Abū Dāwūd in *al-Sunan*, 2:16 §1582.

الصَّدَقَةُ تُطْفِئُ الْـخَطِيئَةَ كَمَـا يُطْفِئُ الْـمَـاءُ النَّارَ.

Charity wipes out sin like water extinguishes fire.[1]

Q.9. What warning has been given to those who do not pay the zakah?

A: A serious warning has been given by the Qur'ān and hadith regarding those who do not pay the zakah. Allah ﷻ states:

﴿وَلَا يَحْسَبَنَّ ٱلَّذِينَ يَبْخَلُونَ بِمَآ ءَاتَىٰهُمُ ٱللَّهُ مِن فَضْلِهِۦ هُوَ خَيْرًا لَّهُمۖ بَلْ هُوَ شَرٌّ لَّهُمۖ سَيُطَوَّقُونَ مَا بَخِلُواْ بِهِۦ يَوْمَ ٱلْقِيَـٰمَةِۗ وَلِلَّهِ مِيرَٰثُ ٱلسَّمَـٰوَٰتِ وَٱلْأَرْضِۗ وَٱللَّهُ بِمَا تَعْمَلُونَ خَبِيرٌ﴾

And those who are niggardly in giving away (from the wealth) which Allah has bestowed upon them out of His bounty must never consider this miserliness of any benefit to themselves; it is rather injurious to them. Soon on the Day of Resurrection, this wealth they are niggardly about will be put around (their necks) like a neck-fetter. To Allah belongs the heritage of the heavens and the earth (i.e., He will remain the Owner of the universe after your death in the same way as He owns it today). And Allah is well aware of all your deeds.[2]

Abū Hurayra relates that the Holy Prophet ﷺ said:

مَنْ آتَاهُ اللهُ مَالًا فَلَمْ يُؤَدِّ زَكَاتَهُ مُثِّلَ لَهُ يَوْمَ الْقِيَامَةِ شُجَاعٌ أَقْرَعُ لَهُ

[1] Narrated by al-Tirmidhī in *al-Jāmiʿ al-Ṣaḥīḥ*, 5:13 §2616.
[2] Qur'ān 3:180.

زَبِيبَتَانِ، فَيَأْخُذُ بِلِهْزِمَتِهِ، وَيَقُولُ: أَنَا مَالُكَ، أَنَا كَنْزُكَ.

Whoever Allah has blessed with wealth, yet he did not pay its zakah, then, on the Day of Judgement his wealth will be presented to him in the shape of a bald-headed poisonous male snake with two poisonous glands in its mouth and it will encircle itself round his neck and bite him over his cheeks and say, "I am your wealth; I am your treasure."[1]

Q.10. What will become of those who do not pay the zakah on gold and silver on the Day of Judgment?

A: A serious warning has been given for those who do not pay the zakah on gold and silver. It is narrated from Abū Hurayra that the Holy Prophet ﷺ said:

مَا مِنْ صَاحِبِ ذَهَبٍ وَلاَ فِضَّةٍ لاَ يُؤَدِّي مِنْهَا حَقَّهَا إِلاَّ إِذَا كَانَ يَوْمُ الْقِيَامَةِ صُفِّحَتْ لَهُ صَفَائِحَ مِنْ نَارٍ فَأُحْمِيَ عَلَيْهَا فِي نَارِ جَهَنَّمَ فَيُكْوَى بِهَا جَنْبُهُ وَجَبِينُهُ وَظَهْرُهُ كُلَّمَا بَرَدَتْ أُعِيدَتْ لَهُ فِي يَوْمٍ كَانَ مِقْدَارُهُ خَمْسِينَ أَلْفَ سَنَةٍ حَتَّى يُقْضَى بَيْنَ الْعِبَادِ فَيَرَى سَبِيلَهُ إِمَّا إِلَى الْجَنَّةِ وَإِمَّا إِلَى النَّارِ.

Whoever possesses gold or silver and does not pay what is due on him, when the Day of Judgement comes, plates of fire would be beaten out for him; these would then be heated in the fire of Hell and his sides, his forehead and his

[1] Narrated by al-Bukhārī in *al-Ṣaḥīḥ*, 2:508 §1338 and 4:1663 §4289; Aḥmad b. Ḥanbal in *al-Musnad*, 2:355 §8646; and al-Nasā'ī in *al-Sunan*, 5:39 §2482.

> back would be cauterised with them. Whenever these cool down, (the process is) repeated during a day the extent of which would be fifty thousand years, until judgment is pronounced among servants, and he sees whether his path is to take him to Paradise or to Hell.[1]

Q.11. WHAT IS THE ISLAMIC CONCEPT OF OWNERSHIP?

A: There is no denying the fact that every economic system in the world is actually based on the concept of ownership. The concept of ownership determines the foundational principles of that economic system alongside other details; and through it, its effectiveness is determined. Therefore the concept of ownership holds a foundational status in any economic system.

An individual's ownership over an item comes into being by the existence of the following two rights:

1. Right of possession
2. Right of disposal

Likewise someone who possesses the above mentioned rights over an item becomes its owner and that item is considered to be his or her property. In fact this is also Islam's concept of ownership which is to benefit and let others benefit.

According to the above discussion the definition of ownership (*milkiya*) can be: 'The ability to take control of something and to do with it as desired'.

In the Islamic concept of ownership, these proprietary rights, to some extent, have been accepted to be purely an individual right—whether someone wishes to associate another person in its joint ownership, the Shariah does not interfere with it. However, the usufructuary right

---

[1] Narrated by Muslim in *al-Ṣaḥīḥ*, 2:680 §987.

(*intifāʿ*), that is the benefit to be attained from the item, is not limited to the individual alone; limiting it as an individual right is to go against the Shariah. If the benefit of a particular property is limited to the individual, like the way ownership is, then the Shariah would not have obligated the zakah on peoples' wealth and assets. This obligation does not stem from shared ownership or use of property, but from mutual benefit. Generally, usufructuary rights are the right of the society and community, whereas proprietary rights are seen as the right of the individual. This is supported by the following Qurʾānic verses.

﴿لِّلرِّجَالِ نَصِيبٌ مِّمَّا تَرَكَ ٱلْوَٰلِدَانِ وَٱلْأَقْرَبُونَ وَلِلنِّسَآءِ نَصِيبٌ مِّمَّا تَرَكَ ٱلْوَٰلِدَانِ وَٱلْأَقْرَبُونَ مِمَّا قَلَّ مِنْهُ أَوْ كَثُرَ نَصِيبًا مَّفْرُوضًا ﴿٧﴾ وَإِذَا حَضَرَ ٱلْقِسْمَةَ أُو۟لُوا۟ ٱلْقُرْبَىٰ وَٱلْيَتَـٰمَىٰ وَٱلْمَسَـٰكِينُ فَٱرْزُقُوهُم مِّنْهُ وَقُولُوا۟ لَهُمْ قَوْلًا مَّعْرُوفًا﴾

Men have a share in (the assets) that their parents and nearest kin leave behind, and women (also) have a share in the inheritance of their parents and the nearest kin. Be it small or large, the share has been fixed (by Allah). If the relatives (other than heirs) and the orphans and the indigent are present on the occasion of the division (of inheritance), give them also something out of it and say to them good and nice words.[1]

[1] Qurʾān 4:7-8.

﴿يَقُولُ أَهْلَكْتُ مَالًا لُّبَدًا ۝٦ أَيَحْسَبُ أَن لَّمْ يَرَهُۥٓ أَحَدٌ ۝٧ أَلَمْ نَجْعَل لَّهُۥ عَيْنَيْنِ ۝٨ وَلِسَانًا وَشَفَتَيْنِ ۝٩ وَهَدَيْنَٰهُ ٱلنَّجْدَيْنِ ۝١٠ فَلَا ٱقْتَحَمَ ٱلْعَقَبَةَ﴾

(Boasting,) he says: 'I have spent heaps of wealth.' Does he think that no one has seen him (making this extravagant spending)? Have We not made for him two eyes? And (have We not given him) a tongue and two lips? And (have We also not) shown him the two highways (of good and evil)? But he has not yet attempted the steep ascent (of the Din [Religion]) of truth and the practical life dedicated to good and piety).[1]

Therefore, the Islamic concept of ownership is unique in letter and spirit and it is the basic foundational stone of the Islamic economic system, which sets it apart from other economic systems. Thus it is definitely at the top of the list in guaranteeing prosperity for humanity.

Q.12. Why should people be made to share their hard-earned wealth through Zakah?

A: It is a common complaint by affluent people that those who are economically broken are themselves to blame for their poverty, and their reliance upon others—albeit the poverty is leading those people to sell their chastity. The affluent generally assume that they bear no responsibility towards the poor. As a result they want to leave them in their pitiful state, whilst remaining busy in protecting their religiosity and outward piety. The Qur'ān has strongly condemned such self-concocted religious ideals, where one is concerned only about himself and his

[1] Ibid., 90:6-11.

personal virtues whilst not striving to lift the needy out of their economic inactivity. If they remain oblivious to them, they should not assume that their behaviour to be virtuous or religious, but it is tantamount to rejecting the *dīn*.

In the same way if someone considers their earnings to be their personal property without any need to share it with others, or that their wealth should be limited to their personal needs and comfort and others should not be allowed to benefit from it (in that their legal rights are not fulfilled), then this will be known as hoarding wealth, which is *ḥarām* and deserving of the Hellfire—even if the wealth is earned lawfully. The Qurʾān states:

﴿يَـٰٓأَيُّهَا ٱلَّذِينَ ءَامَنُوٓاْ إِنَّ كَثِيرًا مِّنَ ٱلْأَحْبَارِ وَٱلرُّهْبَانِ لَيَأْكُلُونَ أَمْوَٰلَ ٱلنَّاسِ بِٱلْبَـٰطِلِ وَيَصُدُّونَ عَن سَبِيلِ ٱللَّهِ ۗ وَٱلَّذِينَ يَكْنِزُونَ ٱلذَّهَبَ وَٱلْفِضَّةَ وَلَا يُنفِقُونَهَا فِى سَبِيلِ ٱللَّهِ فَبَشِّرْهُم بِعَذَابٍ أَلِيمٍ ۝٣٤ يَوْمَ يُحْمَىٰ عَلَيْهَا فِى نَارِ جَهَنَّمَ فَتُكْوَىٰ بِهَا جِبَاهُهُمْ وَجُنُوبُهُمْ وَظُهُورُهُمْ ۖ هَـٰذَا مَا كَنَزْتُمْ لِأَنفُسِكُمْ فَذُوقُواْ مَا كُنتُمْ تَكْنِزُونَ﴾

O believers! Indeed, the majority of the priests and monks (of the People of the Book) devour the wealth of people through unfair (means) and hinder from the path of Allah (i.e., fill their safes with people's money, and hinder it from being spent for the publicity and promotion of the true Din [Religion]). And those who hoard silver and gold and do not spend it in the cause of Allah, warn them of a grievous torment. The Day when this (gold, silver and wealth) will be heated in the Fire of Hell, their foreheads, sides and backs will be branded with this (heated material, and it will be said to them:) 'This is the same (wealth) that you treasured for (the benefit of) your souls. So taste (this wealth) which you had been amassing.'[1]

This subject has been discussed in *Sūra al-Ḥashr*. Allah ﷻ says:

﴿مَّآ أَفَآءَ ٱللَّهُ عَلَىٰ رَسُولِهِۦ مِنْ أَهْلِ ٱلْقُرَىٰ فَلِلَّهِ وَلِلرَّسُولِ وَلِذِى ٱلْقُرْبَىٰ وَٱلْيَتَـٰمَىٰ وَٱلْمَسَـٰكِينِ وَٱبْنِ ٱلسَّبِيلِ كَىْ لَا يَكُونَ دُولَةًۢ بَيْنَ ٱلْأَغْنِيَآءِ مِنكُمْ ۚ وَمَآ ءَاتَىٰكُمُ ٱلرَّسُولُ فَخُذُوهُ وَمَا نَهَىٰكُمْ عَنْهُ فَٱنتَهُوا۟ ۚ وَٱتَّقُوا۟ ٱللَّهَ ۖ إِنَّ ٱللَّهَ شَدِيدُ ٱلْعِقَابِ﴾

And whatever (materials of fay—spoils) Allah restored to His Messenger ([blessings and peace be upon him] taking out) from the people of (the towns captured without war in addition to those of Qurayza, Nadir, Fadak, Khaybar and 'Urayna) belong to Allah and His Messenger (blessings and peace be upon him) and (the Messenger's) near relatives (i.e., Banu Hashim and Banu 'Abd al-Muttalib) and the orphans and the needy and the wayfarer (of society at large. This distribution system is to ensure) that (the whole wealth) may not circulate (only) amongst the rich of you (but should circulate amongst all the classes of society). And whatever the Messenger (blessings and peace be upon him) gives you, take that and whatever he forbids you, abstain (from that) and keep fearing Allah (i.e.,

---

[1] Ibid., 9:34-35.

never scoff at the Messenger's distribution and award). Surely, Allah is Severe to punish.[1]

Q.13. IS THE AVAILABILITY OF WEALTH DEPENDENT UPON THE PROSPERITY OF OTHERS?

A: Yes. The availability of wealth is dependent on the prosperity of others; but for this it is vital that Islam's concept of ownership must be understood in the current circumstances. The commonly understood concepts of ownership have been taken from the Capitalist and Communist ideologies. Islam's economic thought is totally different to those based upon Capitalism and Communism. Whatever Allah ﷻ has created in this world, He has done so for the betterment and prosperity of mankind. Therefore, whatever is present in the shape of wealth, property and assets etc., has the purpose of bettering the human condition. Allah ﷻ states in the Qur'ān:

﴿هُوَ ٱلَّذِى خَلَقَ لَكُم مَّا فِى ٱلْأَرْضِ جَمِيعًا﴾

He is the One Who created for you all that is in the earth.[2]

This concept that everything is created for the betterment of humanity is further clarified at another place in the Qur'ān:

﴿وَأَمَّا مَا يَنفَعُ ٱلنَّاسَ فَيَمْكُثُ فِى ٱلْأَرْضِ﴾

But what is beneficial to the people endures in the earth.[3]

---

[1] Ibid., 59:7.
[2] Ibid., 2:29.
[3] Ibid., 13:17.

It is known from these verses that only those things remain which are beneficial for people. Thus the basis of a things continuance, according to the Qur'ān, is nothing other than that it should have an aspect of being beneficial to humanity in one way or another.

Western science has given the world the concept of 'survival of the fittest', in which only that thing continues to exist which is suited to its environment. In stark opposition to this, the concept presented by Islam is on the basis of what gives benefit and advantage to mankind. History bears witness to the fact that the Companions and Successors, and the early Muslims in general, would only pursue a life of grandeur and opulence in order to bring benefit to others. All of them neglected their personal interests and struggled to benefit others up to the extent that they would sacrifice their own lives in saving another's life.

In Islamic history, there is a renowned incident known as the Battle of Yarmouk, where a few of those who sacrificed their lives for Islam were severely wounded. Ḥudhayfa al-ʿAdawī narrates that in the battle his cousin was seriously wounded and screamed out to him in excruciating pain; so he took water to him. He was about to drink the water when he heard someone else scream out of pain and anguish. Ḥudhayfa al-ʿAdawī's cousin moved his mouth away and signalled him to go towards that direction. When Ḥudhayfa al-ʿAdawī went over there he saw that it was Hishām b. al-ʿĀṣ, the brother of ʿAmr b. al-ʿĀṣ. He asked him if he wanted water so Hishām signalled in affirmation. Water had not yet reached the lips of Hishām who was taking his last breath when he heard someone else crying out in pain. This embodiment of sacrifice signalled to Ḥudhayfa al-ʿAdawī to go over there first. Before Ḥudhayfa al-ʿAdawī could reach the third person, he saw that he had passed away. He went back to Hishām b. al-ʿĀṣ and saw that he passed away too. Then he ran back to his cousin and saw that his soul had too departed.[1]

In this way the three martyrs, who were the embodiment of steadfastness and sacrifice, gave up their own lives by giving preference to others; none of them dared to take a sip of water to soothe their dry throats before his brother could do so. By sacrificing their lives they presented a practical demonstration of the following verse:

﴿وَيُؤْثِرُونَ عَلَىٰٓ أَنفُسِهِمْ وَلَوْ كَانَ بِهِمْ خَصَاصَةٌۚ وَمَن يُوقَ شُحَّ نَفْسِهِۦ فَأُوْلَـٰٓئِكَ هُمُ ٱلْمُفْلِحُونَ﴾

And prefer them to themselves, even though they may themselves be in dire need. And he who is saved from the miserliness of his (ill-commanding) self, it is they who are successful and victorious.[2]

The principle of benefiting others does not apply solely upon Muslims, but applies to Muslims and non-Muslims equally. An incident mentioned in Islamic history in this regard is the most excellent and unrivalled example of this.

During the time of the Holy Prophet ﷺ, water from all the wells of Medina was undrinkable. There was a well owned by a Jew at a distance of four miles from Medina who sold his water at an exorbitant price. The inhabitants of Medina were forced to undertake a tough journey to buy the water from him. Unfortunately he would charge

---

[1] Narrated by Ibn al-Mubārak in *Kitāb al-jihād*, p.97 §116; al-Qurṭubī in *al-Jāmiʿ li-aḥkām al-Qurʾān*, 18:28; and Ibn ʿAsākir in *Tārīkh Dimashq al-kabīr*, 38:180.

[2] Qurʾān 59:9.

the Muslims more than his co-religionists. When the Holy Prophet ﷺ saw the dire state of the Muslims, he gathered all the Companions and said, 'Who from amongst you wants to buy Paradise from my hands?' From the Companions, ʿUthmān b. ʿAffān, who was the wealthiest (thus his title *al-Ghanī*, the wealthy), said, 'I am here at your service.' The Holy Prophet ﷺ said, 'If you buy fifty percent of the well from this Jew and donate it to the Muslims then I will guarantee for you Paradise.' ʿUthmān b. ʿAffān bought a fifty percent stake in the well for 12,000 dirhams and donated it to the Muslims. Now the Muslims had unhindered access to the well and there was plenty of water.

The Holy Prophet ﷺ invited the Jews of Medina to take water from the well after the Muslims had taken what they needed. So the Jews took up this offer from the Holy Prophet ﷺ and opted to take the water free of cost rather than buying it from the Jew. In this way the Jew's business suffered heavy losses and he came to the Holy Prophet ﷺ and said, 'Either, stop providing water for free to the Jews or buy the remaining share of the well from me.' The Holy Prophet ﷺ said that he will not stop providing the Jews the water, but if they could they would buy the remaining share of the well. Thus, ʿUthmān b. ʿAffān following the Holy Prophet's instruction bought the remaining share of the well for 8,000 dirhams and donated it to the inhabitant of Medina.[1]

This incident also clarifies the Islamic concept of ownership that at the heart of its economic philosophy is the desire for the betterment and prosperity of mankind. When the Muslims adopted the values of philanthropy

---

[1] Narrated by al-Bukhārī in *al-Ṣaḥīḥ*, 2:829; al-Tirmidhī in *al-Jāmiʿ al-Ṣaḥīḥ*, 5:627 §3703; al-Nasāʾī in *al-Sunan*, 6:235 §3608; Ibn al-Qayyim in *Zād al-maʿād*, 5:805; al-Ḥalabī in *al-Sīra al-Ḥalabiyya*, 2:268; and al-Shawkānī in *Nayl al-awṭār*, 5:241.

and altruism they were bestowed with such glory that the East and West were under their dominance. When the Muslims began to lose these values, their glory slowly began to slip away from their hands and they were thus relegated to the annals of history.

Q.14. What is meant by basic necessities? Do they change according to changes in time and place?

A: Basic necessities (*al-ḥawā'ij al-aṣliyya*) are in fact related to one's personal needs. These personal needs can naturally change according to a difference in time and place. In order to implement economics rulings upon society at the individual and collective level, it is imperative that limits are set for spending. Through a gradation system, it should be clear how much each individual and institution is permitted to spend and to what extent. Taking into the account the obligatory (*farḍ*), imperative (*wājib*), recommended (*mustaḥabb*), reprehensible (*makrūh*) and forbidden (*ḥarām*) rulings of the Shariah, the system of gradation for spending limits can be produced with six grades.

A table of these six grades are as follows:

Grade	Shariah Ruling	Verdict
Absolute Needs	Obligatory	Permissible
Necessities	Imperative	Permissible
Facilities	Recommended	Permissible
Embellishments	Indifferent	Permissible
Superfluities	Reprehensible	Impermissible
Extravagances	Forbidden	Impermissible

I. ABSOLUTE NEEDS

Absolute needs (*ḥājāt*) are those needs without which it is not possible to live. These are the fundamental rights of every individual and it is obligatory (*farḍ*) upon the state to provide these. There are three fundamental rights which come under absolute needs:

i. Food and water
ii. Clothes
iii. Accommodation

The following saying of the Holy Prophet ﷺ emphasises upon the importance of these basic necessities:

لَيْسَ لابْنِ آدَمَ حَقٌّ سِوَى هَذِهِ الْخِصَالِ: بَيْتٌ يَسْكُنُهُ، وَثَوْبٌ يُوَارِي عَوْرَتَهُ، وَجِلْفُ الْخُبْزِ وَالْمَاءِ.

> There is no (absolute) right for the children of Ādam except these: a house to reside in; clothes to cover his body; and adequate amount of bread and water.[1]

II. NECESSITIES

After the absolute needs the second grade is of necessities (*ḍarūriyāt*). These are things without which one can stay alive, but life would be very agonising and unbearable. If everyone in society has their absolute needs fulfilled then it is obligatory upon the state to provide people with their necessities. In today's world, electricity, water, gas, education and healthcare are such necessities without which human life cannot function properly. This is why

[1] Narrated by al-Tirmidhī in *al-Jāmiᶜ al-Ṣaḥīḥ*, 30:571 §2341; al-Ḥākim in *al-Mustadrak*, 4:374 §7866; ᶜAbd b. Ḥumayd in *al-Musnad*, 1:46 §46; and al-Bayhaqī in *Shuᶜab al-īmān*, 5:157 §680.

they are considered imperative (*wājib*) according to the ruling of the Shariah.

III. Facilities and Amenities

Facilities and amenities (*tashīlāt*) are those requirements which are necessary in order to live a comfortable life. They include means of transport (car, motorbike, etc.), access to the media (T.V., radio, etc.), among others. In an Islamic society, the Shariah rules them as recommended (*mustaḥabb*). Therefore, if people purchase these through their lawful incomes, then it is their right.

IV. Embellishments and Decorations

Embellishments and decorations (*taḥsīnāt*) is the utilisation of resources for mere comfort. They have no link with the basic necessities of life. If however, someone has a lawful income and fulfils the rights of his dependants, it is permissible (*mubāḥ*) for him to spend on the embellishments and decorations.

V. Superfluities

Superfluities (*isrāfāt*) refers to such spending which is unnecessary and not for mere comfort, but to show-off one's wealth. This has been declared reprehensible (*makrūh*) in the Shariah. An example of this is the pointless customs that people adhere to, where huge amounts are squandered. Similarly, excessive exhibition of wealth in order to show one's social stature also falls within such category.

VI. Extravagance

Extravagance (*tabdhīrāt*) refers to that wasteful and extravagant spending where the function is to merely exhibit wealth and to seek excessive pleasure. The wealth being spent in this manner is in actual fact surplus wealth which is more than the required amount for any individual; such wealth has been declared by the Holy Prophet ﷺ as the right of those people who are economically deprived. Therefore, whoever deprives such people of their right and wastes this wealth in frivolous entertainment and pleasure will not be forgiven for this act, as it has been declared forbidden (*ḥarām*) by the Shariah. Preventing such squandering of wealth is the responsibility of the state.

It must be noted that the jurists have classified professional tools and equipment, defensive weapons, and clothing related to the different seasons as falling under basic necessities (*al-ḥawāʾij al-aṣliyya*) which come under one's personal matters. Naturally there will be a difference of opinion on this, as such things are related to changes in one's time and place. The standard of dress will change according to one's circumstances; likewise, means of transport will differ. All of these however will come under one's basic necessities.

Although the line drawn by the jurists between the needs and comfort must be adhered to while determining the degree of the rulings, it must be kept in mind that the zakah is to be utilised upon the poor and destitute. Therefore, the boundaries for the basic necessities (*al-ḥawāʾij al-aṣliyya*) must not be so broad that affluent people are considered as eligible to receive zakah.

Q.15. What is the best method of paying zakah?

A: The best way to pay zakah is that from the eight categories mentioned in the Qur᾿ān, one first pays the zakah to one's poor and eligible relations, neighbours, acquaintances, colleagues and residents of one's community before paying it to others. In the same way those people who do not themselves ask for alms although they are poor due to their self-respect and dignity should be sought after and given the zakah. If these people are needier than the above mentioned eligible categories then they should figure at the top of the list.

Other than this it is not permissible to pay the zakah as a service or a reward however it is permissible to buy something with zakah money and distribute it amongst the poor and destitute.

Q.16. Does Islam give priority to collectiveness over individuality?

A: In the *dīn* of Islam, collectiveness has been given priority over individuality because Islam is not only a *dīn* of individual practice but a *dīn* of collectivity. With the exception of the first pillar, the five pillars of Islam teach the lessons of collectivity. This is explained below.

I. Ritual Prayer

In terms of reward and other benefits, praying in congregation is superior to praying alone although concentration and contemplation is more likely to be attained offering the ritual prayer as an individual in a closed room. Allah ﷻ has declared that prayer in congregation is superior and more rewarding to praying alone, and has declared collective practice to be superior to individual practice. Similarly, the Friday prayer is more rewarded due to collectiveness, and the same is the case with the *ʿĪd* prayer. So collectiveness has been given priority over individuality.

II. FASTING

This is such a practice in which collectiveness is not possible as fasting is a personal act, but Allah ﷻ has also included a collective element in it. In the holy month of *Ramaḍān*, the Muslims come together for the *ṣuḥūr* and *ifṭār* meals. Furthermore, the act of preparing a meal for people to break their fast has been declared as rewarding. In the night, the Muslims assemble in the mosques to offer the *tarāwīḥ* ritual prayer; it was the *Sunna* of the Holy Prophet ﷺ to offer this prayer in congregation. So the fasting during the day and the ritual prayer in the night has combined both individual and collective elements in the act of fasting.

III. ZAKAH

Zakah is a financial act of worship which has both individual and collective aspects associated with it. However Allah ﷻ has preferred collectiveness over individuality. Therefore, if the zakah can be utilised through social welfare projects rather than individual contributions, it would be much better at eradicating poverty from society. We see that those families that were dependent upon zakah ten or twenty years ago are still in need of zakah today. Therefore, there is little benefit in paying the zakah at an individual level as it does not fulfil the social requirements of the *dīn*. Like other practices, the zakah also has an aspect of collectiveness which is dominant over individuality.

IV. Pilgrimage

This is all in all a collective practice and cannot be carried out individually. Allah ﷻ gathers everyone in the plain of ʿ*Arafāt*. The circumambulation of the *Ka*ʿ*ba* is performed collectively as is the *sa*ʿ*y* between *al-Ṣafā* and *al-Marwa*. Likewise the *wuqūf* at ʿ*Arafāt* and *Muzdalifa* is also a collective action. Similarly the ritual sacrifice is performed by everyone. All who come to the Pilgrimage proclaim the words, '*labbayk Allāhumma labbayk*' in unison. So the pilgrimage to the Sacred House of Allah has also been endorsed as a collective practice. The Qurʾān states:

﴿وَأَذِّن فِى ٱلنَّاسِ بِٱلْحَجِّ يَأْتُوكَ رِجَالًا وَعَلَىٰ كُلِّ ضَامِرٍ يَأْتِينَ مِن كُلِّ فَجٍّ عَمِيقٍ﴾

> *And proclaim the Hajj (Pilgrimage) aloud amongst the people. They will approach you on foot and (mounted) on all lean camels, coming by distant tracks.*[1]

If the above mentioned pillars of Islam are analysed carefully then it becomes clear that although there is an aspect of individuality in all practices, there is also an element of collectiveness which is superior. In some cases there is no individuality at all.

Q.17. Is it superior to fulfil zakah individually or collectively?

A: There are two ways of paying zakah, one is individually and the other is collectively. Whether zakah is paid individually or through collective planning, both will be beneficial. However with regards to far reaching outcomes, paying zakah to collective projects is far more

---

[1] Qurʾān 22:27.

beneficial. An example of this is that paying zakah individually is paying it to a single poor person. Adding a little collectiveness to this is to pay it to the whole family. If a little zakah is paid to the whole family, then that family will prosper. Therefore, rather than spending zakah on a single individual, it is better to bring benefit to the economic affairs of the whole family.

However, going further than this, if the zakah is collected by the treasury or through some collective planning a means of income is created by giving a lump of sum to a family so that they no longer remain in need of zakah but may even be able to pay the zakah in the future. For example, if women from these eligible families are taught sewing and embroidery and are provided with sewing machines and some cash in order for them to start their business, in this way those women will be able to earn a respectable living and they will not be reliant on hand-outs. In the same way small businesses can be set up through micro-financing which will enable people to earn a respectable living from home.

Therefore, if the payment of zakah is done under a collective planning rather than it being paid individually, the fate of poor families will begin to permanently change. In this way, according to Allah ﷻ and Islam, collectivity has been held superior to individual practice. Planning takes place in collective practices and this planning can change the fate of an entire nation—as was the case under the government of ʿUmar b. ʿAbd al-Azīz when there was not a single person who was eligible to receive zakah. A study of Islamic history points out that during the government of the Holy Prophet ﷺ and the Rightly Guided Caliphs, the institution of zakah was under the control of the government which used to centrally collect and distribute the zakah. This is the reason why a wide range of benefits and far reaching results were obtained from zakah money.

Q.18. What are the *Maṣārif al-Zakāh*?

A: *Maṣārif* is the plural of *maṣraf*. *Maṣārif* refers to those categories upon which the zakah can be spent. In the following hadith, Ziyād b. Hārith states:

أَمَّرَنِي رَسُولُ ﷺ عَلَى قَوْمِي، فَقُلْتُ: يَا رَسُولَ اللهِ، أَعْطِنِي مِنْ صَدَقَاتِهِمْ، فَفَعَلَ وَكَتَبَ لِي بِذَلِكَ كِتَابًا. فَأَتَاهُ رَجُلٌ، فَقَالَ: يَا رَسُولَ اللهِ، أَعْطِنِي مِنَ الصَّدَقَةِ. فَقَالَ رَسُولُ ﷺ: إِنَّ اللهَ لَمْ يَرْضَ بِحُكْمِ نَبِيٍّ وَلا غَيْرِهِ فِي الصَّدَقَاتِ، حَتَّى حَكَمَ فِيهَا هُوَ مِنَ السَّمَاءِ، فَجَزَّأَهَا ثَمَانِيَةَ أَجْزَاءٍ، فَإِنْ كُنْتَ مِنْ تِلْكَ الأَجْزَاءِ أَعْطَيْتُكَ مِنْهَا.

The Holy Prophet ﷺ appointed me as the head of my people. I said, 'O Messenger of Allah, give me some of their charity.' The Holy Prophet ﷺ did this and also gave me a written statement regarding it. Then another person also came to the Holy Prophet ﷺ and also requested, 'O Messenger of Allah, provide me with some money from the charity.' The Holy Prophet ﷺ said, 'Allah ﷻ does not like the (personal) decision of a Prophet or anyone else until He reveals a ruling Himself. Allah ﷻ has divided the recipients of zakah into eight categories. If you are also from these categories then I will give you money from the zakah.'[1]

Q.19. WHICH CLASSES OF PEOPLE ARE ELIGIBLE TO RECEIVE ZAKAH?

A: According to the Qur'ān, there are eight categories that are eligible to receive zakah. Allah ﷻ states:

﴿إِنَّمَا ٱلصَّدَقَٰتُ لِلْفُقَرَآءِ وَٱلْمَسَٰكِينِ وَٱلْعَٰمِلِينَ عَلَيْهَا وَٱلْمُؤَلَّفَةِ قُلُوبُهُمْ وَفِى ٱلرِّقَابِ وَٱلْغَٰرِمِينَ وَفِى سَبِيلِ ٱللَّهِ وَٱبْنِ ٱلسَّبِيلِ ۖ فَرِيضَةً مِّنَ ٱللَّهِ ۗ وَٱللَّهُ عَلِيمٌ حَكِيمٌ﴾

Indeed, alms (Zakat) are meant for the poor and the indigent, and those who are deployed to collect charities and those in whose hearts the inculcation of love for Islam is aimed at. And, (moreover, spending Zakat for the) freeing of human lives (from the yoke of slavery) and removing the burden of those who are to pay debt and (those who toil hard) in the cause of Allah and the wayfarers (is true). This (all) has been prescribed by Allah, and Allah is All-Knowing, Most Wise.[2]

In light of the above verses, the following eight are the categories of zakah:

1. The poor (*fuqarā'*)
2. The destitute (*masākīn*)
3. The collectors of zakah (*ʿāmilīn*)
4. To soften the hearts of people (*mu'allafa al-qulūb*)

---

[1] Narrated by Abū Dāwūd in *al-Sunan*, 2:117 §1630; al-Ṭaḥāwī in *Sharḥ maʿāni al-āthār*, 2:65 §2937; and al-Bayhaqī in *Sunan al-kubrā*, 4:173 §7522.
[2] Qur'ān 9:60.

5. The slaves (*riqāb*)
6. The debtors (*ghārimīn*)
7. Those in the path of Allah (*fī sabīl Allāh*)
8. The travellers (*ibn sabīl*)

Q.20. WHAT IS A *FAQĪR*?

A: According to the jurists, a *faqīr* is such a person who has some belonging through which his basic needs can be met, but it amounts to below the threshold level (*nisāb*). This is the first category of those eligible to receive zakah.

It is narrated by ʿAbd Allāh b. ʿAbbās that when the Holy Prophet ﷺ sent Muʿādh b. Jabal to Yemen, he guided him that Allah ﷻ has made zakah obligatory upon the Muslims which is to be taken from the wealthy and given to the poor.[1]

Q.21. WHAT IS A *MISKĪN*?

A: A *miskīn* is poorer than a *faqīr* and is thus needier. This is the second category of zakah. A *miskīn* like a *faqīr* is also dependant on others. Abū Hurayra narrates that the Holy Prophet ﷺ said:

لَيْسَ الْـمِسْكِينُ الَّذِي تَرُدُّهُ الأُكْلَةُ وَالأُكْلَتَانِ، وَلَكِنِ الْـمِسْكِينُ الَّذِي لَيْسَ لَهُ غِنًى وَيَسْتَحْيِي أَوْ لَا يَسْأَلُ النَّاسَ إِلْحَافًا.

> The poor person is not the one who asks a morsel or two (of food) from others, but the poor is the one who has nothing and is ashamed to beg.[2]

Q.22. WHO ARE THE *ʿĀMILĪN*?

A: The *ʿāmilīn* are those people who are appointed by the government to collect zakah and *ʿushr* (the tax on crops).

---

[1] Narrated by al-Bukhārī in *al-Ṣaḥīḥ*, 2:505 §1331.
[2] Ibid., 2:538 §1409.

They will be paid a salary from the zakah fund irrespective if they are rich or poor.

ʿAbd Allāh b. al-Saʿdī narrates:

أَنَّهُ قَدِمَ عَلَى عُمَرَ فِي خِلاَفَتِهِ فَقَالَ لَهُ عُمَرُ أَلَـمْ أُحَدَّثْ أَنَّكَ تَلِي مِنْ أَعْمَالِ النَّاسِ أَعْمالاً، فَإِذَا أُعْطِيتَ الْعُمالَةَ كَرِهْتَهَا. فَقُلْتُ بَلَى. فَقَالَ عُمَرُ مَا تُرِيدُ إِلَى ذَلِكَ قُلْتُ إِنَّ لِي أَفْرَاسًا وَأَعْبُدًا، وَأَنَا بِخَيْرٍ، وَأُرِيدُ أَنْ تَكُونَ عُمالَتِي صَدَقَةً عَلَى الْـمُسْلِمِينَ. قَالَ عُمَرُ لاَ تَفْعَلْ فَإِنِّي كُنْتُ أَرَدْتُ الَّذِي أَرَدْتَ فَكَانَ رَسُولُ اللهِ يُعْطِينِي الْعَطَاءَ فَأَقُولُ أَعْطِهِ أَفْقَرَ إِلَيْهِ مِنِّي. حَتَّى أَعْطَانِي مَرَّةً مَالاً فَقُلْتُ أَعْطِهِ أَفْقَرَ إِلَيْهِ مِنِّي. فَقَالَ النَّبِيُّ خُذْهُ فَتَمَوَّلْهُ وَتَصَدَّقْ بِهِ، فَما جَاءَكَ مِنْ هَذَا الْـمَـالِ وَأَنْتَ غَيْرُ مُشْرِفٍ وَلاَ سَائِلٍ فَخُذْهُ، وَإِلاَّ فَلاَ تُتْبِعْهُ نَفْسَكَ.

When he went to ʿUmar during his Caliphate, ʿUmar said to him, "Haven't I been told that you do certain jobs for the people but when you are given payment you refuse to take it?" ʿAbd Allāh added: I said, "Yes." ʿUmar said, "Why do you do so?" I said, "I have horses and slaves and I am living in prosperity and I wish that my payment should be kept as a charitable gift for the Muslims." ʿUmar said, "Do not do so, for I intended to do the same as you do. Allah's Messenger ﷺ used to give me gifts and I used to say to him, 'Give it to someone needier than me.' Once he gave me some money and I said, 'Give it to someone needier than me,' whereupon the Prophet ﷺ said, 'Take it and keep it in your possession and then give it in charity. Take whatever comes to you of this money if you are not keen to have it and not asking for it; otherwise (i.e., if it does not come to you) do not seek to have it yourself."[1]

Q.23. What is meant by *Mu'allafa al-Qulūb*?

A: This is the fourth category eligible to receive zakah. The purpose of this is to financially assist those who are fiercely opposed to Islam in order that their opposition to Islam can be extinguished. This also includes those selected non-Muslims who can be brought closer to Islam by being supported financially in order that they embrace Islam. This also includes the financial support of those who have newly converted to Islam so that their financial difficulty does not force them to revert back to disbelief.

Ṣafwān b. Umayya narrates: "The Holy Prophet ﷺ gave some property to me on the day of the Battle of *Ḥunayn*, although at that time he was the most disliked person in my view. He continued to grant me until he became the most beloved to me."[2]

We can find numerous examples of this in the life of the Holy Prophet ﷺ where he would give financial assistance to various tribes and families to soften their hearts towards Islam. Anas b. Mālik narrates:

أَنَّ رَجُلاً سَأَلَ النَّبِيَّ ﷺ غَنَمًا بَيْنَ جَبَلَيْنِ فَأَعْطَاهُ إِيَّاهُ فَأَتَى قَوْمَهُ فَقَالَ أَيْ قَوْمِ أَسْلِمُوا فَوَاللهِ إِنَّ مُحَمَّدًا لَيُعْطِي عَطَاءً مَا يَخَافُ الْفَقْرَ.

A man asked the Holy Prophet ﷺ to given him a very large flock between two mountains and he gave it to him. He returned to his tribe and said:

---

[1] Narrated by al-Bukhārī in *al-Ṣaḥīḥ*, 6:2620 §6744; Aḥmad b. Ḥanbal in *al-Musnad*, 1:17 §100 and 1:21 §136; and al-Nasā'ī in *al-Sunan*, 5:104 §2607.

[2] Narrated by al-Tirmidhī in *al-Jāmiʿ al-Ṣaḥīḥ*, 3:53 §666.

> 'O my people! Enter into Islam, for by God Muhammad gives so much he does not fear poverty.'

Anas stated that the person entered into Islam for no other reason except for the world, but after he became a Muslim Islam became dearer to him than the world and all that it contains.[1]

Q.24. WHAT IS A *RIQĀB*?

A: *Riqāb* literally means necks and is used in the meaning to free slaves. This is the fifth category of those eligible to receive zakah. The zakah can be used to free slaves. ᶜAbd Allāh b. ᶜAbbās narrates:

يُعْتِقُ مِن زَكَاةِ مَالِهِ.

> A person can free a slave from his zakah money.[2]

Before Islam, the institution of slavery was prevalent in most of the world. Weak, needy, and poor people were enslaved by powerful people. Similarly, as a result of wars, the dominant party would enslave the defeated people and take ownership of their homes, land, and even their lives. Islam took a gradual approach to bring an end to slavery: it created legal and moral avenues for setting slaves free. The Muslims were encouraged to use their wealth to invite slave owners, who were unwilling to let go of their slaves for free, to forgo their ownership. Islam also gave a slave the right to earn his freedom; this is known as *badl al-kitāba*. The slave would be freed on the payment of the desired amount which could be paid using one's zakah money.

---

[1] Narrated by Muslim in *al-Ṣaḥīḥ*, 4:1806 §2312; and al-Bayhaqī in *al-Sunan al-kubrā*, 7:19 §12,967.
[2] Al-Qurṭubī, *al-Jāmiᶜ li aḥkām al-Qurʾān*, 4:185.

Q.25. WHAT IS A *GHĀRIM*?

A: This is the sixth category of those eligible to receive zakah. *Ghārim* refers to someone who is in debt. Zakah money can be used to pay off debt. Anas b. Mālik narrates that the Holy Prophet ﷺ said:

> إِنَّ الْـمَسْأَلَةَ لَا تَحِلُّ إِلَّا لِثَلَاثَةٍ: لِذِي فَقْرٍ مُدْقِعٍ، أَوْ لِذِي غُرْمٍ مُفْظِعٍ، أَوْ لِذِي دَمٍ مُوْجِعٍ.
>
> It is not permitted for anyone to beg except in three situations: a destitute who is in dire poverty; a person heavily in debt; and the one who has to pay blood money.[1]

Qabīṣa b. Mukhāriq states:

> تَحَمَّلْتُ حَمَالَةً فَأَتَيْتُ رَسُولَ ا ﷺ أَسْأَلُهُ فِيهَا فَقَالَ: أَقِمْ حَتَّى تَأْتِيَنَا الصَّدَقَةُ فَنَأْمُرَ لَكَ بِهَا. قَالَ ثُمَّ قَالَ: يَا قَبِيصَةُ إِنَّ الْـمَسْأَلَةَ لَا تَحِلُّ إِلاَّ لأَحَدِ ثَلاَثَةٍ رَجُلٍ تَحَمَّلَ حَمَالَةً فَحَلَّتْ لَهُ الْـمَسْأَلَةُ حَتَّى يُصِيبَهَا ثُمَّ يُمْسِكُ وَرَجُلٍ أَصَابَتْهُ جَائِحَةٌ اجْتَاحَتْ مَالَهُ فَحَلَّتْ لَهُ الْـمَسْأَلَةُ حَتَّى يُصِيبَ قِوَامًا مِنْ عَيْشٍ - أَوْ قَالَ سِدَادًا مِنْ عَيْشٍ - وَرَجُلٍ أَصَابَتْهُ فَاقَةٌ حَتَّى يَقُومَ ثَلاَثَةٌ مِنْ ذَوِي الْحِجَا مِنْ قَوْمِهِ لَقَدْ أَصَابَتْ فُلاَنًا فَاقَةٌ فَحَلَّتْ لَهُ الْـمَسْأَلَةُ حَتَّى يُصِيبَ قِوَامًا مِنْ عَيْشٍ - أَوْ قَالَ سِدَادًا مِنْ عَيْشٍ - فَمَا سِوَاهُنَّ مِنَ الْـمَسْأَلَةِ يَا قَبِيصَةُ سُحْتًا يَأْكُلُهَا صَاحِبُهَا سُحْتًا.

---

[1] Narrated by Aḥmad b. Ḥanbal in *al-Musnad*, 3:126 §12,300; Abū Dāwūd in *al-Sunan*, 2:120 §1641; Ibn Mājah in *al-Sunan*, 2:740 §2198; and al-Ṭayālasī in *al-Musnad*, 1:285 §2145.

> I was under debt and I came to the Messenger of Allah ﷺ and begged from him regarding it. He said: 'Wait till we receive charity, so that we order that to be given to you.' He again said: 'Qabīṣa, begging is not permissible but for one of three people: one who has incurred debt, for him begging is permissible till he pays that off, after which he must stop it; a man whose property has been destroyed by a calamity which has smitten him, for him begging is permissible till he gets what will support life, or will provide him reasonable subsistence; and a person who has been smitten by poverty, the genuineness of which is confirmed by three intelligent members of his community, for him begging is permissible till he gets what will support him, or will provide him subsistence. Qabīṣa, besides these three, begging (for any other reason) is forbidden, and the one who engages in such consumes that what is unlawful.'[1]

Q.26. What does *fī sabīl Allāh* mean?

A: *Fī sabīl Allāh* refers to those who are on the path of Allah. This is the seventh category of those eligible to receive zakah. There is a difference of opinion among the jurists on the implication of the term '*fī sabīl Allāh*'. Imam al-Kāsānī al-Ḥanafī states:

> *Fī sabīl Allāh* refers to all virtuous acts that achieve divine proximity. This includes everyone who struggles for virtuous acts and the obedience to Allah while they are eligible to receive zakah.[2]

---

[1] Narrated by Muslim in *al-Ṣaḥīḥ*, 2:722 §1044.

[2] Al-Kāsānī, *Badāʾiʿ al-ṣanāʾiʿ*, 2:45.

Q.27. WHAT DOES *IBN AL-SABĪL* MEAN?

A: *Ibn al-sabīl* literally means the 'son of the road'; it simply refers to travellers. This is the eighth category of those eligible to receive zakah. A traveller who is affluent in his home land, but becomes needy whilst travelling, can be assisted through the money specified for zakah.

Abū Saʿīd al-Khudrī narrates that the Holy Prophet ﷺ said:

لَا تَحِلُّ الصَّدَقَةُ لِغَنِيٍّ إِلَّا فِي سَبِيلِ اللهِ أَوِ ابْنِ السَّبِيلِ، أَوْ جَارٍ فَقِيرٍ يُتَصَدَّقُ عَلَيهِ فَيُهْدِي لَكَ، أَوْ يَدْعُوكَ.

> Charity is not permitted for an affluent person except if he is on the path of Allah or a traveller. If a poor neighbour, who is given charity, gifts you something or invites you for dinner (it is permissible to accept his gifts and to accept his invitation).[1]

Imam al-Kāsānī clarifying the status of *ibn al-sabīl* writes:

> This refers to that person who is far away from his resources and home. He can be assisted by money specified for zakah even if such a person is wealthy in his own city as he is in need at that time.[2]

Q.28. WHAT IS THE *NIṢĀB*?

A: For those resources, assets, wealth, money and property upon which zakah is obligatory, there is a specific amount which this personal wealth must exceed

---

[1] Narrated by Aḥmad b. Ḥanbal in *al-Musnad*, 3:97 §11,948; Abū Dāwūd in *al-Sunan*, 2:119 §1637; and al-Bayhaqī in *al-Sunan al-kubrā*, 7:22 §12,978.

[2] Al-Kāsānī, *Badāʾiʿ al-ṣanāʾiʿ*, 2:46.

for zakah to become obligated. This specific amount is known as *niṣāb*.

Q.29. What is the *niṣāb* of gold?

A: Zakah is obligatory (*farḍ*) on gold according to the modern measurement of 87.48 grams—not on an amount less than this. ʿAlī b. Abī Ṭālib narrates that the Holy Prophet ﷺ said:

لَيْسَ عَلَيْكَ شَيْءٌ يَعْنِي فِي الذَّهَبِ حَتَّى تَكُونَ لَكَ عِشْرُونَ دِينَارًا. فَإِذَا كَانَتْ لَكَ عِشْرُونَ دِينَارًا وَحَالَ عَلَيْهَا الْحَوْلُ فَفِيهَا نِصْفُ دِينَارٍ، فَمَا زَادَ فَبِحِسَابِ ذَلِكَ.

> Nothing is obligatory upon you with regards to gold until it reaches twenty dinars. When you have in your possession twenty dinars and a whole year has passed, then there is (zakah of) half a dinar; and whatever exceeds it, then (the zakah is) in accordance to that.[1]

It is narrated from both ʿAbd Allāh b. ʿUmar and ʿĀʾisha al-Ṣiddīqa that the Holy Prophet ﷺ used to take zakah of half a dinar from twenty dirhams, and one dinar from every forty dinars (i.e., $^{1}/_{40}{}^{th}$).[2]

It should be noted that those days a dinar was a gold cold which weighed 87.48 grams.

Q.30. What is the *niṣāb* of silver?

A: Zakah is obligatory (*farḍ*) on silver which amounts to 612.36 grams and not on amount less than it. It is

---

[1] Narrated by Abū Dāwūd in *al-Sunan*, 2:100 §1573; and al-Bayhaqī in *al-Sunan al-kubrā*, 4:137 §7325.

[2] Narrated by Ibn Mājah in *al-Sunan*, 1:571 §1791.

obligatory to pay one-fortieth of the zakatable amount. Abū Saʿīd al-Khudrī states that the Holy Prophet ﷺ said:

لَيْسَ فِيمَا دُونَ خَمْسِ أَوَاقٍ مِنَ الْوَرِقِ صَدَقَةٌ.

> Zakah is not obligatory to be paid on any silver less than five *awqiya* (amounting to 612.36 grams).[1]

It must be kept in mind that the zakah is paid at a rate of 2.5%, either according to the weight or value.

Q.31. Is the zakah payable on valuable stones and gems?

A: If the valuable stones are for trading purposes, they will be zakatable. Otherwise if they are for personal use, there is no zakah to be paid on them irrespective of their value.

Q.32. Is the zakah obligatory upon a non-Muslim?

A: The zakah is only obligatory upon Muslims. This is one of the conditions of zakah. If an apostate returns to Islam, the zakah will not be obligated on the interim period of disbelief.

Q.33. What is the ruling on stock market shares with regard to zakah?

A: Shares will also be included with the rest of the assets and wealth in order to calculate whether or not it is above

---

[1] Narrated by al-Bukhārī in *al-Ṣaḥīḥ*, 2:529 §1390; Muslim in *al-Ṣaḥīḥ*, 2:675 §980; Aḥmad b. Ḥanbal in *al-Musnad*, 3:86 §11,831; al-Nasāʾī in *al-Sunan*, 5:36 §2474; and Mālik in *al-Muwaṭṭaʾ*, 1:244 §578.

the *niṣāb*. If it is above the *niṣāb*, the zakah will become obligatory and will thus have to be paid.

There is no doubt that it is permitted to buy and sell shares of companies that engage in lawful trade. Trading (*muḍāraba* – a type of trading) is permitted on shares which can either make a profit or a loss. As shares are bought for two purposes, both purposes have different rulings with regards to zakah. These two purposes of buying shares are discussed below.

I. Buying shares in a company on a profit and loss basis

If shares are bought in a company with the aim of gaining the company's profit then the zakah is as follows: after the passing of a whole year, from the total shares, a portion that would represent the building and machinery is to be deducted, and the remaining shares that would represent commodities, good and capital are those which zakah is to be paid upon.

II. Buying and selling shares as trade goods (capital goods)

If shares are bought on the outset with the intention of selling them when the price rises, as the shares are brought in the capacity of trade goods the zakah must be paid on the full value of the shares. There will be no deduction of shares representing machinery and the building because they do not represent tools or means of trading, but will represent trade goods, so cannot be excluded. Any money, currency, bank accounts, bonds, deposits, silver, gold and trade goods that are in the ownership of a Muslim trader, qualify for zakah to be paid on their value. When paying zakah on silver, gold and trade goods their value at the time of paying zakah must be used in calculating zakah and not their purchase value. So it is better for a Muslim trader to carry out a stock check and evaluate in order to work out the actual value of goods. Besides the factory which is being used for production purposes, the land which it is on, the building, equipment related to production and the cost of machinery are not subject to zakah. However a Muslim trader has to pay zakah upon all the raw materials, finished goods and all products that are sent to the market for sale.

Most of the time traders are involved in buying and selling with pending payments to be made and received. Other than the trading, people have personal loans owed to them. Thus at the time of calculating the zakah, those payments or loans that are due to be received should be included into the total wealth liable for zakah; and those loans or payments that are to be paid out should be deducted from it. The remainder is the total wealth upon which zakah is due.

Q.34. Which value should be used to calculate zakah upon shares?

A: Whether shares are bought on a profit and loss basis or for capital gain, in both cases the zakah will be calculated upon the market value of the shares. The purchase value of the shares will not be taken into consideration at all, irrespective if the value of the shares has increased or decreased at the time of paying the zakah.

Q.35. What is the ruling upon paper currency that is above the *niṣāb*?

A: The zakah is obligatory (*farḍ*) upon paper currency that is above the *niṣāb*. The jurists have given the following conditions for the zakah to be obligatory on paper currency:

1. The currency should amount to the *niṣāb* (of either the value of gold or silver).
2. It has been in one's possession for one lunar year.
3. It should be free of debt.
4. The paper currency is surplus of one's basic necessities, such as one's daily expenditure, clothing, accommodation, etc.

Q.36. Is the zakah due on houses, flats or land which are used as accommodation?

A: Zakah is not due upon a house, flat or land which is being used as personal accommodation. However, if a house, flat or shop is being rented out, the annual profit gained from them after the expenses are deducted will be added to the owner's annual profit; and if the annual profits from all means of income reach the *niṣāb*, then the zakah will be paid on them.

Zakah must be paid upon the value of all houses, flats and land that are used for business or trade purposes. Again the purchase price is not taken into account but the market value of the day. This point is one to be pondered over by those who invest in land, and buy and sell property.

Zakah upon the deposit that is paid as a guarantee in renting a property must be paid by the tenant. In the same way the zakah for security deposit that are paid by traders or agencies to firms or organisations that are returnable, must be paid by the depositor.

Q.37. What is referred to as trade goods?

A: Those items that are purchased for the purpose of resale (in order to gain a profit) are termed as trade goods. Examples are, such as grain, cloth, domestic appliances and various types of animals, etc.

Q.38. Is the zakah obligatory upon trade goods and equipment?

A: The zakah is obligatory (*farḍ*) upon trade goods but not upon professional tools and equipment used in trade. Trade tools are a means of income and means of income have been exempted from zakah by the Shariah. There will however be zakah due on the profits earned by their use considering the fact that it reaches the *niṣāb* and a year has passed.

Q.39. What is the method of working out the zakah due upon trade goods?

A: The zakah will be calculated upon estimating the annual value of trade goods. The value of these goods must be put together with the rest of the assets, money and jewellery etc., and then the zakah is to be calculated. Besides these, those pending payments to be received upon goods sold on credit, if they are in the form of cash and their payment date has expired or they are new loans pending to be repaid, in both cases the loans are expected to be repaid and thus all of those loans will be zakatable. If the loan is payable in the form of trade goods and its payment is expected then the value of those goods must be calculated and added to the total zakatable sum in order to work out the zakah due to be paid.

Q.40. What is the method of calculating the zakah in the business of buying and selling cars?

A: In order to pay the zakah, the total value of all the cars must be calculated. Then any loan which has been given out and is expected to be returned should also be added to the amount. If any loan is to be paid then the amount of that loan should be separated from the total amount. Then the zakah should be paid at the rate of 2.5% on the remaining sum. If the value of the cars is less than the *niṣāb* for some part of the year or during the same year more cars are purchased taking their value to or above the *niṣāb* then the year is to be considered to begin at the point when the *niṣāb* was reached, and the previous period will not be included.

Q.41. How will the zakah be paid in a business partnership?

A: In a business partnership each partner will pay the zakah upon their share of the business. For example, if two people are equal partners in a business then after a lunar year has passed each will pay the amount in accordance to his or her business share. It is narrated by Anas b. Mālik that Abū Bakr al-Ṣiddīq wrote with regards to the rulings of zakah:

> Any assets that are shared, they should work out the proportionate amount and pay the zakah accordingly.[1]

Q.42. Is the obligation of zakah fulfilled by paying income tax?

A: The obligation of zakah is not lifted by paying income tax. The reason for this is that the zakah is an obligatory (*farḍ*) practice of the Shariah and is considered an act of worship, whereas tax is void of such notions. For instance, making a formal intention (*niyya*) is a precondition of zakah which is not the case with tax. The second reason is that the amount to be paid as zakah is

[1] Narrated by al-Bukhārī in *al-Ṣaḥīḥ*, 2:526 §1383.

determined by the Shariah, whilst in tax this is not the case. The third reason is that zakah is established as a permanent right, whereas tax is not so. The zakah is spent upon the eight categories mentioned in the Quran, whereas tax is spent on governmental projects. The zakah has spiritual, moral, human and collective aims whereas tax does not have these targets amongst its aims.

Q.43. WHAT IS *MĀL AL-ḌIMĀR*?

A: *Māl al-ḍimār* is that belonging which is no longer in one's possession and there is no chance of regaining it. For example the possession may be lost, stolen, confiscated, or the borrower may refuse to return it.

Q.44. IS ZAKAH DUE ON *MĀL AL-ḌIMĀR*?

A: One does not have to pay zakah on *māl al-ḍimār* because there is no complete ownership over the possession. However, if one regains custody of the lost property, even if it is after many years, then the zakah for that year must be paid.

Q.45. IS THE ZAKAH DUE ON JEWELLERY OTHER THAN SILVER AND GOLD?

A: No. The zakah is not due on jewellery that is made for personal use out of material other than silver and gold.

Q.46. IF THERE IS SOME GOLD AND SILVER, WILL THE ZAKAH BECOME OBLIGATORY IF THEY ARE MERGED TOGETHER?

A: In this case the value of one can be considered to be the other and both the values can be merged together. If either of the silver or gold reaches the *niṣāb*, then the zakah must be paid accordingly. If neither reach the *niṣāb*, then no zakah is due.

This issue is discussed in the books of *fiqh* and it comes under the subject of *ḍamm* (integration/merging); this points out which items can be merged together in order to reach the *niṣāb*. For example, the zakah is not due on less than five camels, thirty cows and forty goats. If all these three types of animals are owned and all three are less than the *niṣāb*, and there is no gold, silver or cash, then there is consensus that they cannot be merged together. That is if the value of all the three types of animals are added together and it does not reach the *niṣāb* for one of the animals, zakah is not obligatory. However, the ruling on bulls, cows and buffaloes is the same, so it is permissible to merge them together to reach the *niṣāb* value. ʿAllāma Ibn Hammām al-Ḥanafī writes:

وَالسَّوَائِمُ الْـمُخْتَلِفَةُ الْـجِنْسِ لَا تُضَمُّ بِالْإِجْمَاعِ كَالْإِبِلِ وَالْغَنَمِ.

وَالنَّقْدَانِ يُضَمُّ أَحَدُهُمَا إِلَى الْآخَرِ فِي تَكْمِيلِ النِّصَابِ.

> Animals which are of different genera, such as camels and goats, cannot be merged together by consensus. One (type of) currency will be merged with another in order to reach the *niṣāb*.[1]

It is also the dominant opinion that silver can be added to gold and vice versa in order for the *niṣāb* to be reached. Furthermore trade goods will also be added for this purpose. This position is also more compatible with the wordings of the hadith. Bukayr b. ʿAbd Allāh al-Ashajj narrates:

مَضَتِ السُّنَّةُ مِنْ أَصْحَابِ رَسُولِ الله بِضَمِّ الذَّهَبِ إِلَى الْفِضَّةِ،

وَالْفِضَّةُ إِلَى الذَّهَبِ لِإِخْرَاجِ الزَّكَاةِ.

---

[1] Ibn Hammām, *Sharḥ Fatḥ al-Qadīr*, 2:221.

> It was the practice of the Companions of the Messenger of Allah ﷺ that in working out the zakah they would add gold to silver and silver to gold in order to pay the zakah.[1]

Q.47. If someone does not possess gold and silver but has currency excess of his basic necessities, will it be obligatory on him to pay zakah? If so, what is the method of paying it?

A: After fulfilling one's basic necessities, if there is money and other surplus assets other than gold and silver, zakah will be obligatory. Gold and silver were the currency in the time of the Holy Prophet ﷺ. In the present era, paper currency has replaced precious metals, so paying zakah on all forms of currency alongside gold and silver is more beneficial to the poor and hence must be paid.

The method of calculating the zakah is that any surplus currency that remains after fulfilling one's basic necessities, if it comes to the value of 52.5 tolas[2] (612.36 grams) of silver, and a whole lunar year has passed and there is no debt to pay, the zakah must be paid at the rate of 2.5%.

Q.48. Which is used for *niṣāb*: gold or silver?

A: According to Imam Abū Ḥanīfa the one which is more beneficial for the poor should be used.[3] In other words, if one has wealth which reaches the *niṣāb* of either of gold or silver, one should use the one which brings greater benefit to the poor. So if the *niṣāb* of silver has been

---

[1] Al-Kāsānī, *Badāʾiʿ al-ṣanāʾiʿ*, 2:19.
[2] One tola equals 11.663 grams. Ed.
[3] Al-Kāsānī, *Badāʾiʿ al-ṣanāʾiʿ*, 2:21.

reached, but not of gold, the zakah will be obligated as it brings greater benefit. Imam al-Marghinānī al-Ḥanafī states:

يُقَوِّمُهَا بِمَا أَنْفَعُ لِلْمَسَاكِينِ احْتِيَاطًا لِحَقِّ الْفُقَرَاءِ.

> It should be valued according to what is more beneficial for the poor and destitute, as a measure of caution for the rights of the poor.[1]

He writes further:

وَتَفْسِيرُ الْأَنْفَعِ: أَنْ يُقَوِّمَهَا بِمَا يَبْلُغُ نِصَابًا.

> The interpretation of 'more beneficial' is that the gold and silver are valued (in such a way) that the value reaches the *niṣāb*.[2]

ʿAllāma Ḥaṣkafī al-Ḥanafī states:

وَلَوْ بَلَغَ بِأَحَدِهِمَا نِصَابًا وَخُمُسًا وَبِالْآخَرِ أَقَلَّ، قَوَّمَهُ بِالْآخَرِ نَفْعًا لِلْفَقِيرِ.

> If the *niṣāb* and *khumus* are reached by either one of them (i.e., gold and silver) and the other one is less than it, the one which is more beneficial to the poor will be used.[3]

What this means is, if one has enough money to buy either gold or silver equal to the *niṣāb*, the zakah will become obligatory.

ʿAllāma Ibn Hammām al-Ḥanafī states:

---

[1] Al-Marghinānī, *al-Hidāya*, 1:105.
[2] Ibid.
[3] Ḥaṣkafī, *al-Durr al-mukhtār*, 2:299.

لَوْ كَانَ يُقَوِّمُهُ بِأَحَدِ النَّقْدَيْنِ يَتِمُّ النِّصَابُ وَبِالْآخَرِ لَا. فَإِنَّهُ يُقَوِّمُهُ بِمَا يَتِمُّ بِهِ النِّصَابُ بِالِاتِّفَاقِ.

If the wealth reaches the *niṣāb* for one of the two (either gold or silver), then there is unanimity that it would be considered to reach the *niṣāb* even if it does not reach it for the other.[1]

Q.49. Can the zakah be paid before it is due?

A: The zakah can be paid before its due and this is one of the acceptable methods of paying it. ʿAlī b. Abī Ṭālib narrates that ʿAbbās asked the Holy Prophet ﷺ whether it was permissible to pay the zakah before it is due, and the Holy Prophet ﷺ permitted him to do it.[2]

Q.50. On the passing of a whole year, if the zakah has not been paid and all the wealth is lost, what is the ruling in this case?

A: In such a case the zakah is not liable to be paid for that period.

Q.51. After the passing of a year, if all the wealth is spent in the way of Allah, what will be the ruling in this case?

A: If after the passing of a whole year all the wealth and assets are spent in the path of Allah, the zakah due is pardoned. If it is however lost on purpose, then the owner will be held accountable just as is the case with a trust; in such scenario he will have to pay the zakah. It should be noted that if the assets are lost in a natural disaster the owner will not be held accountable.

---

[1] Ibn Hammām, *Sharḥ Fatḥ al-Qadīr*, 2:220.

[2] Narrated by Abū Dāwūd in *al-Sunan*, 2:115 §1624.

Q.52. If the zakah is due by someone but that person dies before paying it, how should it be paid?

A: If zakah is due by someone who has died, the zakah will be taken from his or her wealth or estate that is left behind (if the deceased instructed it through his or her will). If no instruction was left, the zakah cannot be taken in this way. However if the guardians of the deceased pay the zakah from his or her wealth, that is best. So the zakah can be paid from the wealth left behind by the deceased in this way.

Q.53. Can the zakah be paid in advance through installments during the year?

A: Yes. Someone who is obligated to pay the zakah can pay money to the needy through instalments during the year with the intention of paying zakah. When the year comes to an end, the zakah should be calculated and the remaining balance should be paid. The remaining balance can likewise be paid in instalments.

Q.54. Can the zakah of two years be paid together at the same time?

A: It is best to pay zakah on time; however if there is zakah due from the previous year, it can be paid with the zakah of the present year.

Q.55. If zakah is unknowingly paid to someone who is not eligible to receive it, will the obligation be fulfilled?

A: If the zakah is unknowingly paid to someone who is not eligible to receive it, the obligation of the zakah will be fulfilled. However, before paying the zakah an effort should be made to determine whether those receiving zakah money are eligible to receive it. Abū Hurayra narrates that the Holy Prophet ﷺ said:

قَالَ رَجُلٌ: لَأَتَصَدَّقَنَّ بِصَدَقَةٍ فَخَرَجَ بِصَدَقَتِهِ فَوَضَعَهَا فِي يَدِ
سَارِقٍ فَأَصْبَحُوا يَتَحَدَّثُونَ تُصُدِّقَ عَلَى سَارِقٍ فَقَالَ: اللَّهُمَّ لَكَ
الْحَمْدُ لَأَتَصَدَّقَنَّ بِصَدَقَةٍ فَخَرَجَ بِصَدَقَتِهِ فَوَضَعَهَا فِي يَدَيْ زَانِيَةٍ
فَأَصْبَحُوا يَتَحَدَّثُونَ تُصُدِّقَ اللَّيْلَةَ عَلَى زَانِيَةٍ فَقَالَ: اللَّهُمَّ لَكَ
الْحَمْدُ عَلَى زَانِيَةٍ لَأَتَصَدَّقَنَّ بِصَدَقَةٍ فَخَرَجَ بِصَدَقَتِهِ فَوَضَعَهَا فِي
يَدَيْ غَنِيٍّ فَأَصْبَحُوا يَتَحَدَّثُونَ تُصُدِّقَ عَلَى غَنِيٍّ فَقَالَ: اللَّهُمَّ لَكَ
الْحَمْدُ عَلَى سَارِقٍ وَعَلَى زَانِيَةٍ وَعَلَى غَنِيٍّ فَأُتِيَ فَقِيلَ لَهُ أَمَّا صَدَقَتُكَ
عَلَى سَارِقٍ فَلَعَلَّهُ أَنْ يَسْتَعِفَّ عَنْ سَرِقَتِهِ وَأَمَّا الزَّانِيَةُ فَلَعَلَّهَا أَنْ
تَسْتَعِفَّ عَنْ زِنَاهَا وَأَمَّا الْغَنِيُّ فَلَعَلَّهُ يَعْتَبِرُ فَيُنْفِقُ مِمَّا أَعْطَاهُ اللهُ.

A man (from amongst the people before you) said: 'Indeed! I will give in charity.' So he took his charity out and placed it in a thief's hand. In the morning the people were talking (about this incident) and saying: 'Charity was given to a thief last night.' The man said: 'O Allah! Praise be to You. I have given charity to a thief. Indeed, I will give in charity!' So he took his charity out and he placed it in a prostitute's hand. In the morning the people were talking (about this incident) and saying: 'Charity was given to a prostitute last night.' On hearing this, the man said: 'Praise be to You, O Allah! I gave charity to a prostitute. Indeed, I will give in charity!' So he took his charity out and placed it in a rich man's hand. In the morning the people were talking (about this incident) and saying: 'Charity was given to a rich man last night.' The man said: 'O Allah! Praise be to You (for helping me) give charity to a thief, a prostitute and a rich man.' Then he had a dream in which he was told that his charity to the thief might result in his refraining from his theft, his charity to the prostitute might help her abstain from her immorality, and his charity to the rich man might help him pay heed and spend from what Allah had bestowed upon him.[1]

Q.56. What kind of wealth, asset, property must zakah be paid on?

A: It is obligatory to pay zakah upon four types of assets:

1. Gold, silver and money.
2. Animals such as camels, cows and goats, etc.
3. All kinds of trade goods.
4. Those products that are produced from the land such as fruits, vegetables and minerals, etc.

Q.57. Does unlawful earnings become pure by paying the zakah?

A: No, paying zakah does not purify unlawful (*ḥarām*) earnings. The charity given from unlawful earnings is not accepted by Allah ﷻ as is the case with the supplication made by a person with unlawful income. Abū Hurayra narrates that the Holy Prophet ﷺ said:

مَنْ تَصَدَّقَ بِعَدْلِ تَمْرَةٍ مِنْ كَسْبٍ طَيِّبٍ وَلَا يَقْبَلُ اللهُ إِلَّا الطَّيِّبَ
وَإِنَّ اللهَ يَتَقَبَّلُهَا بِيَمِينِهِ ثُمَّ يُرَبِّيهَا لِصَاحِبِهِ كَمَا يُرَبِّي أَحَدُكُمْ فَلُوَّهُ

[1] Narrated by al-Bukhārī in *al-Ṣaḥīḥ*, 2:516 §1355; Muslim in *al-Ṣaḥīḥ*, 2:709 §1022; and al-Nasā'ī in *al-Sunan*, 5:55 §2523.

حَتَّى تَكُونَ مِثْلَ الْجَبَلِ.

> If one gives in charity what equals one date-fruit from money which is earned lawfully, and Allah only accepts money which is earned honestly, Allah takes it in His right (hand) and then enlarges its reward for that person (who has given it), as anyone of you brings up his baby horse, so much so that it becomes as big as a mountain.[1]

At the end of the narration given by Imam Muslim, Abū Hurayra states:

ثُمَّ ذَكَرَ الرَّجُلَ يُطِيلُ السَّفَرَ أَشْعَثَ أَغْبَرَ يَمُدُّ يَدَيْهِ إِلَى السَّمَاءِ يَا رَبِّ يَا رَبِّ وَمَطْعَمُهُ حَرَامٌ وَمَشْرَبُهُ حَرَامٌ وَمَلْبَسُهُ حَرَامٌ وَغُذِيَ بِالْحَرَامِ فَأَنَّى يُسْتَجَابُ لِذَلِكَ.

> He then made a mention of a person who travels widely, his hair dishevelled and covered with dust. He lifts his hand towards the sky (and thus makes the supplication): "O Lord, O Lord," whereas his diet is unlawful, his drink is unlawful, and his clothes are unlawful and his nourishment is unlawful. How then can his supplication be accepted?[2]

Similarly in another narration Abū Hurayra states that the Holy Prophet ﷺ said:

---

[1] Narrated by al-Bukhārī in *al-Ṣaḥīḥ*, 2:511 §1344 and 6:2706 §6993; Aḥmad b. Ḥanbal in *al-Musnad*, 2:331 §8363 and 2:381 §8948; al-Tirmidhī in *al-Jāmiʿ al-Ṣaḥīḥ*, 3:69 §661; al-Nasāʾī in *al-Sunan*, 5:57 §2525; and Ibn Mājah in *al-Sunan*, 1:590 §1842.

[2] Narrated by Muslim in *al-Ṣaḥīḥ*, 2:702 §1014.

إِذَا أَدَّيْتَ الزَّكَاةَ فَقَدْ قَضَيْتَ مَا عَلَيْكَ، وَمَنْ جَمَعَ مَالًا حَرَامًا ثُمَّ تَصَدَّقَ بِهِ لَمْ يَكُنْ لَهُ فِيهِ أَجْرٌ، وَكَانَ إِصْرُهُ عَلَيْهِ.

> When you have paid the zakah from your property, you have fulfilled your obligation. The person who gathers unlawful earnings and then donates it as charity, he will receive no reward from it and he will be answerable for the burden of the act.[1]

These narrations make it clear that it is not permissible to give charity from one's unlawful earnings. If the earnings are from a source which has been declared unlawful by the Qur'ān and Sunna through definitive sources, such as usury for example, it will not be permitted for one to give it as charity.

If someone takes something illegally, the only way to recover from this is to find the owner of that item, or its inheritors, and to return it to the rightful owner. If the owner cannot be found then the item should be donated to the poor on behalf of the owner with the intention of making right the wrong. This intention will have a reward.

Q.58. Who is not eligible to receive zakah?

A: The following people cannot receive zakah:

1. A wealthy person, i.e., someone upon whom it is obligatory to pay zakah or has some assets that are the value of *niṣāb* and in surplus of the basic necessities. For example, if someone has copper cutlery which is surplus to their need and their value is that of *niṣāb*, then it is not permitted for that

[1] Narrated by Ibn Khuzayma in *al-Ṣaḥīḥ*, 8:110 §2471; Ibn Ḥibbān in *al-Ṣaḥīḥ*, 5:11 §3216; al-Ḥākim in *al-Mustadrak*, 1:547 §1440; and al-Bayhaqī in *al-Sunan al-kubrā*, 4:84 §7032.

person to receive zakah, although it is not *wājib* for that person to pay zakah on that excess cutlery.

2. Relations such as parents, grandparents, etc.
3. Children, nephew, nieces, and grandchildren.
4. Spouse
5. The children of a wealthy person who are below the age of puberty, as children under the age of puberty are to be catered for by their guardian.

Q.59. Is it necessary to inform the person receiving zakah that it is zakah?

A: It is not necessary to inform the person who is receiving zakah that he is receiving zakah. It is also permissible to give zakah under the title of a prize or as an ᶜ*Īd* gift for poor children.

Q.60. Is it permissible to pay zakah to the Banū Hāshim?

A: In the early period it was not permissible for the Banū Hāshim to receive zakah as they received *khumus*. As now the *khumus* no longer exists it is also permissible for them to receive zakah. So if Banū Hāshim are eligible to receive zakah they can be given it. However, it is best to maintain the respect and dignity of the Banū Hāshim; the rulers and top officials should make separate arrangements for the assistance of the needy members of Banū Hāshim.

Q.61. Can the zakah be paid to those who sin openly?

A: Yes, until the open sinner remains in the fold of Islam and does not harm the Muslims, he can be given zakah. The reason for this is that if the zakah can be taken from those who are sinful and disobedient, it should surely be permissible for them to receive it. Furthermore, the hadith below in its generalisation includes openly sinful and disobedient people, that zakah will be taken from the wealthy and distributed among the poor and needy. The Holy Prophet ﷺ said:

تُؤْخَذُ مِنْ أَغْنِيَائِهِمْ وَتُرَدُّ فِي فُقَرَائِهِمْ.

> The zakah is taken from the rich and given to the poor.[1]

Nevertheless the zakah should not be given to open sinners whom it is known that the money will be spent upon sinful practices such as drinking and gambling. In this way the money which is given for the pleasure of Allah should not be spent on carrying out sinful practices; to do so would be to go against the Shariah.

Q.62. Can those who are not eligible to receive zakah be employed as zakah collectors?

A: The later jurists have permitted the appointment of such people as zakah collectors those who are not eligible to receive the zakah. This is because the money they receive will not be given to them as charity but instead it will be their salary.

Q.63. Is the ruling on *ta'līf al-qalb* annulled in this era?

A: One of the eight categories eligible to receive zakah is the *mu'allafa al-qulūb* (to soften the hearts of people). The Holy Prophet ﷺ utilised the zakah and *ʿushr* upon this category and never abrogated it. All payments to this category were brought to an end by the second caliph, ʿUmar b. al-Khaṭṭāb. Some jurists (like the *Ḥanafīs*) are of

[1] Narrated by Abū Dāwūd in *al-Sunan*, 2:18 §1584.

the view that as this category was brought to an end by ʿUmar b. al-Khaṭṭāb and it was witnessed to by the Companions, who did not object to it or refused to comply, it proves that there is a consensus (*ijmāʿ*) amongst the Companions that this category is abrogated; and this counts as a definitive evidence (*al-dalīl al-qaṭʿī*). Other jurists have said that as *taʾlīf al-qalb* (softening the heart) was the need of the time, which is why it remained; but once Islam became powerful there was no longer a need to attract people towards Islam in this fashion, so the ruling was no longer needed.

In the opinion of the author, the need for *taʾlīf al-qalb* (softening the heart) is as necessary today as it was in the beginning of Islam. Today there is also a need to assist the poor and needy from the zakah fund in order to safeguard beliefs. Targeting those people who are vulnerable of being used by the opponents of Islam, converts to Islam, and those who require help through financial assistance should be given in order to facilitate their steadfastness in practicing Islam. Enemy powers can be given financial incentives in order to safeguard Muslim from their evil. As resources are spent upon promoting distorted beliefs, in the same way Islam can utilise resources in the promotion of the truth and inviting people towards the correct beliefs. It is the duty of affluent Muslims and those with political power to propagate the message of Islam to non-Muslims and to assist them financially through the zakah fund.

The consensus (*ijmāʿ*) of the Companions was that there was no longer a need for this category at that time. Today if there is not a need then it is not compulsory to create this category, but if there is a need then zakah can be spent on this category. This was not the abrogation of the Qurʾānic ruling but as the need no longer remained it was no longer implemented—just like *tayammum* can be performed until there is the capacity to use water. The ruling remains as long as the reason for its implementation remains: it can neither be abrogated for good nor can it be implemented continually.

Q.64. Is it permissible to send one's zakah to another locality?

A: It is best to spend zakah where it was collected but according to need or a valid reason it can be spent elsewhere. Rather than distributing it personally it can be deposited into the *bayt al-māl* so that it can be spent upon those needy people who live in other areas. For this purpose the collection of zakah must be overseen by the government as was the case at the time of the Holy Prophet ﷺ and the Rightly Guided Caliphs. Evidence of this point of view can be found in the narration of Muʿādh b. Jabal when he said to the people of Yemen: "You can give materials such as sheets of cloth or other clothing instead of oats and corn, which will be more convenient for you and that will be beneficial for the Companions of the Holy Prophet ﷺ in Medina."[1]

In the contemporary era various organisations are working according to the needs of the time for the collective social and economic welfare of society. If the zakah is donated to the organisations then social welfare can be better achieved and those that are in need can be seen to. This raises the standard of life in society and an environment of social cooperation can be created in all areas at the same time.

---

[1] Narrated by al-Bukhārī in *al-Ṣaḥīḥ*, 2:525.

Q.65. Can a traveller be trusted on his word and be given zakah without any evidence?

A: Accepting the word of a traveller refers to when someone comes and says, 'I am a traveller and I require money to complete my journey.' One can accept this statement as it stands, or make further enquiries to see the truthfulness of this statement. Imam al-Qurṭubī writes:

> With regards to the *dīn* it is necessary that the person proves it, although regarding other attributes the person's physical appearance is sufficient evidence.[1]

The evidence of this is the hadith narrated by Jarīr. He narrates: While we were in the company of the Messenger of Allah ﷺ in the early hours of the morning, some people came there who were barefooted, naked, wearing striped woollen clothes with their swords hung around their necks. Most of them, in fact, all of them, belonged to the tribe of Muḍar. The colour of the face of the Messenger of Allah ﷺ underwent a change when he saw them in poverty. He then entered his house and came out and commanded Bilāl to pronounce *ādhān*. He pronounced *ādhān* and *iqāma*, and the Holy Prophet ﷺ observed prayer along with his Companion and then addressed them reciting verses of the Holy Qurʾān:

﴿يَـٰٓأَيُّهَا ٱلَّذِينَ ءَامَنُواْ ٱتَّقُواْ ٱللَّهَ وَلْتَنظُرْ نَفْسٌ مَّا قَدَّمَتْ لِغَدٍۖ
وَٱتَّقُواْ ٱللَّهَۚ﴾

> *O believers! Keep fearing Allah. And everyone should be vigilant to what he has sent forward*

---

[1] Al-Qurṭubī, *al-Jāmiʿ li aḥkām al-Qurʾān*, 4:187-188.

for tomorrow (the Day of Reckoning). And always fear Allah.[1]

Then the audience began to vie with one another in giving charity. Some donated a dinar, others a dirham, still others clothes, some donated a *ṣāʿ*[2] of wheat, some a *ṣāʿ* of dates; till the Holy Prophet ﷺ said: "Bring even if it is half a date." Then a person from among the Anṣār came there with a money bag which he could not lift. Then the people followed continuously, till I saw two heaps of eatables and clothes, and I saw the face of the Messenger glistening, like gold on account of joy.[3]

It is proven from this hadith that the apparent state of a traveller should be sufficient as the Holy Prophet ﷺ only judged the apparent state and motivated people to give charity. The Holy Prophet ﷺ did not ask for any proof from them, nor did he ask them whether they had any wealth, assets or property.

Q.66. Is the zakah obligatory upon a woman's *mahr* (bridal-gift)?

A: A precondition of zakah to be obligatory (*farḍ*) is complete possession of the item. What needs to be checked is whether the woman has total possession of the

---

[1] Qur'ān 59:18.

[2] Different areas use different measures for *ṣāʿ*. According to each area the weight is different. For instance, the weight of the *ṣāʿ Ḥijāzī* used in the surrounding areas of Mecca and Medina was different to *ṣāʿ ʿIrāqī* that was used in areas surrounding Baghdad and Kufa. The *ṣāʿ ʿIrāqī* is also known as *ṣāʿ Baghdādī*. Similarly, later on, the *ṣāʿ* of ʿUmar b. ʿAbd al-ʿAzīz and the *ṣāʿ* of Hāshmī were also introduced. However according to the common and prevalent measurement, currently half a *ṣāʿ* of wheat would amount to 2.249 kg, whereas half a *ṣāʿ* of oats would be 2.32 kg. According to this a *ṣāʿ* of butter is 4.498 kg and a *ṣāʿ* of oats is 4.64 kg.

[3] Narrated by Muslim in *al-Ṣaḥīḥ*, 2:705 §1017.

mahr (bridal-gift). If the *mahr* is not in her possession, the zakah will not have to be paid.

Q.67. Whose responsibility is it to pay the zakah on the wife's jewellery?

A: From the husband and wife, whoever is the actual owner of the jewellery will be the one who will be liable to pay the zakah. If the husband has given jewellery to his wife to merely use and he actually owns it and can sell them whenever he wants, in this case the zakah will not be due upon the wife but the husband will have to pay it. However, if the wife owns the jewellery herself and has the discretion to wear it and sell it when she wishes then the zakah is due upon her.

Q.68. Can a divorced woman be given zakah by her ex-husband?

A: Yes, a woman who is divorced can be given zakah by her former husband.

Q.69. Can zakah be given to someone to be spent on their wedding?

A: Yes, zakah can be paid to a man or woman in order to pay for their wedding but it must be ensured that the zakah is not spent upon excessiveness or any illegal custom.

Q.70. Can a husband and wife give zakah to each other?

A: No, a husband and wife cannot pay zakah to each other.

Q.71. Can parents give zakah to their children?

A: Parents cannot give zakah to their children because those people who are under one's guardianship, it is *wājib* to provide for them. The zakah cannot be paid to one's dependants, offspring, wife, parents, grandparents, great-grandparents, grandchildren, etc. Apart from these, the zakah can be given to all other relations such as brothers, sisters, aunties, uncles and their children, if they are poor. In fact it is better to give zakah to them than other needy people because the obligation is fulfilled together with keeping good relations with relatives. Double reward is earned by giving zakah to them.

Q.72. Can one's needy parents by given zakah?

A: No, one's needy parents cannot be given zakah. In fact assisting parents physically and financially is an obligation on the children. If children have to pay zakah then they should use their personal resources to assist their needy parents not the money assigned for zakah.

Jābir b. ʿAbd Allāh narrates that a man said, 'O Messenger of Allah, indeed I have both wealth and children, and my father wishes to spend my money on his own needs (and leave nothing for me).' So the Holy Prophet ﷺ said:

أَنْتَ وَمَالُكَ لِأَبِيكَ.

You and your wealth belong to your father.[1]

[1] Narrated by Ibn Mājah in *al-Sunan*, 3:88-89 §2291.

Q.73. Is zakah obligatory on jewellery made for one's children's weddings whilst the children are still under the age of puberty?

A: If the jewellery has been gifted on the name of the children and the children are under the age of puberty, the zakah will not be obligatory on the jewellery. If however the jewellery is on the name of the parents, and they have specific jewellery set aside for each child then zakah is to be paid.

Q.74. Can needy students be assisted by zakah?

A: Yes, education institutes whether they take fees from the students or not, can have a zakah fund by which they meet the needs of poor students. This is in fact very appropriate so that the students can be assisted so that their studies can be pursued with peace of mind.

The jurists have stated:

> A student can receive zakah as he has devoted himself to studying and hence cannot earn a living. Therefore the need for acquiring the basic needs of life makes zakah permissible for him.[1]

So the zakah can be paid to religious education institutes especially to meet the needs of the poor students. Most religious educational institutes and welfare organisations run on zakah. So it is best that the zakah fund is utilised in order to meet the needs of poor students be that in the form of stationary and books, or fees, food, medicine, etc.

---

[1] Ḥaṣkafī, *al-Durr al-mukhtār*, 1:140.

Q.75. Is the zakah due on money that is saved for Pilgrimage?

A: Money saved with the intention of performing the Pilgrimage is not exempted from the zakah. However if the money has been deposited to the government for this purpose then it is exempted from zakah.

Q.76. Is the zakah obligated on someone in debt?

A: Someone who is in debt should put aside the money that is owed and if the remainder reaches the *niṣāb* then it is *wājib* to pay zakah but if it is less than the *niṣāb* then it is not.

Q.77. Can debt be cleared by zakah money?

A: Yes, if the person in debt is poor and does not qualify to pay zakah, there is no doubt his debt can be cleared by zakah money. However, if the person is wealthy and qualifies to pay zakah, it is not permitted for him to receive zakah or get the debt paid off through zakah. In the former case, clearly the person is eligible to receive zakah, so the person who is owed the money does not need to mention to him that he is using zakah money to cancel his debt but just needs to let him know that he no longer needs to pay back the loan so that his dignity and self-respect are not tainted.

Q.78. Can zakah money be used to pay fines due upon prisoners in order to secure their release?

A: For prisoners who are from an affluent background who can afford to pay the fines, it is not permissible to use zakah money to secure their release. However for prisoners who are poor and needy who cannot afford the fines and are to spend lengthy time in prison, zakah money can be used to secure their freedom. These people come under the three categories of those eligible to receive zakah: the *faqīr*, *miskīn* and *riqāb*. Although *al-riqāb* was used in the meaning of slaves at the time of the revelation of the Qur'ān, in contemporary times there is room for it to be used for poor and destitute prisoners.

Q.79. Should zakah and *ṣadaqa* be paid only in *Ramaḍān*?

A: The payment of zakah and *ṣadaqa* is not conditional to the month of *Ramaḍān*. It is *wājib* to pay the zakah as soon as the year has passed and its payment should not be delayed until the month of *Ramaḍān*. However if the month of *Ramaḍān* is near to the time when a year has passed, such as the zakah is due in *Shaʿbān*, then there is no harm in waiting till *Ramaḍān* to pay it. Nevertheless if the year is completed in *Muḥarram* then it is not permissible to wait till *Ramaḍān* to pay the zakah; although, the zakah can be paid in *Ramaḍān* before the completion of the year, which will be in *Muḥarram*. Delaying the payment of zakah from the time that it has become *wājib* is not permitted.

Q.80. What does *infāq fī sabīl Allāh* mean?

A: *Infāq* means 'to spend' and *fī sabīl Allāh* means 'in the path of Allah'. Thus, in the Shariah, *infāq fī sabīl Allāh* means 'to spend in the path of Allah'.

Q.81. What is the reality of spending in the path of Allah?

A: It is to spend one's money and wealth upon the poor and needy so that their economic deadlock is resolved and their creative capacity may be restored in order that they may play their due role in society. A practical example of this is the *muwākhāt* of Medina, which exhibited the practical form of benevolence (*iḥsān*) in accomplishing goals through spending in the path of Allah.

Q.82. What are the Qurʾānic commandments with regards to spending in the path of Allah?

A: The Qurʾān clearly mentions that whatever Allah ﷻ has provided, some of it should be spent in the path of Allah. Some verses are given below.

﴿يَـٰٓأَيُّهَا ٱلَّذِينَ ءَامَنُوٓاْ أَنفِقُواْ مِمَّا رَزَقْنَـٰكُم﴾

O believers! Spend (in the cause of Allah) out of whatever We have provided for you.[1]

﴿يَـٰٓأَيُّهَا ٱلَّذِينَ ءَامَنُوٓاْ أَنفِقُواْ مِن طَيِّبَـٰتِ مَا كَسَبْتُمْ وَمِمَّآ أَخْرَجْنَا لَكُم مِّنَ ٱلْأَرْضِ﴾

O believers! Spend (in the way of Allah) of your lawful and clean earnings and of that which We bring forth for you from the earth.[2]

﴿وَأَنفِقُواْ فِى سَبِيلِ ٱللَّهِ وَلَا تُلْقُواْ بِأَيْدِيكُمْ إِلَى ٱلتَّهْلُكَةِ وَأَحْسِنُوٓاْ إِنَّ ٱللَّهَ يُحِبُّ ٱلْمُحْسِنِينَ﴾

And spend in the cause of Allah; and do not cast yourselves into destruction with your own hands;

[1] Ibid., 2:254.
[2] Ibid., 2:267.

and adopt righteousness. Verily, Allah loves the righteous.[1]

﴿لَن تَنَالُواْ ٱلْبِرَّ حَتَّىٰ تُنفِقُواْ مِمَّا تُحِبُّونَۚ وَمَا تُنفِقُواْ مِن شَيْءٍ فَإِنَّ ٱللَّهَ بِهِۦ عَلِيمٌ﴾

You can never attain to piety unless you spend (in the cause of Allah) out of that which you like the most; and Allah surely knows well whatever you give away.[2]

﴿وَءَاتَى ٱلْمَالَ عَلَىٰ حُبِّهِۦ ذَوِى ٱلْقُرْبَىٰ وَٱلْيَتَٰمَىٰ وَٱلْمَسَٰكِينَ وَٱبْنَ ٱلسَّبِيلِ وَٱلسَّآئِلِينَ وَفِى ٱلرِّقَابِ وَأَقَامَ ٱلصَّلَوٰةَ وَءَاتَى ٱلزَّكَوٰةَ وَٱلْمُوفُونَ بِعَهْدِهِمْ إِذَا عَٰهَدُواْ﴾

Driven by love for Allah, he spends (his) wealth on the kindred, the orphans, the needy, the wayfarers and those who ask and in (liberating slaves') necks, and establishes Prayer and pays Zakat (the Alms-due). And when they make a promise, they fulfil it.[3]

The above verses provide encouragement to spend those blessings given by Allah in His path. So that alongside gaining Allah's pleasure, one's income and earnings may be prosperous and blessed.

---

[1] Ibid., 2:195.
[2] Ibid., 3:92.
[3] Ibid., 2:177.

Q.83. What rulings have been given with regards to spending in the path of Allah in the hadiths?

A: Spending in the path of Allah has been greatly encouraged in the hadiths. In fact there are plenty of practical demonstrations of this in the *sīra*. Some hadiths are mentioned below.

1. Abū Hurayra relates:

أَنَّ رَسُولَ ا ﷺ قَالَ: قَالَ ﷻ: أَنْفِقْ أُنْفِقْ عَلَيْكَ. وَقَالَ: يَدُ اللهِ مَلأَى لاَ تَغِيضُهَا نَفَقَةٌ، سَحَّاءُ اللَّيْلَ وَالنَّهَارَ. وَقَالَ: أَرَأَيْتُمْ مَا أَنْفَقَ مُنْذُ خَلَقَ السَّمَاءَ وَالأَرْضَ فَإِنَّهُ لَمْ يَغِضْ مَا فِي يَدِهِ.

The Holy Prophet ﷺ narrates that Allah ﷻ said, "Spend (O man), and I shall spend on you." He ﷺ also said, "Allah's Hand is full, and (its fullness) is not affected by the continuous spending night and day." He also said, "Do you see what He has spent since He created the Heavens and the Earth? Nevertheless, what is in His Hand is not decreased."[1]

2. In another narration, Abū Hurayra narrates that the Holy Prophet ﷺ said:

مَنْ أَنْفَقَ زَوْجَيْنِ فِي سَبِيلِ اللهِ، نُودِيَ مِنْ أَبْوَابِ الْجَنَّةِ: يَا عَبْدَ اللهِ! هَذَا خَيْرٌ.

---

[1] Narrated by al-Bukhārī in *al-Ṣaḥīḥ*, 4:1724 §4407; Muslim in *al-Ṣaḥīḥ*, 2:690 §993; Aḥmad b. Ḥanbal in *al-Musnad*, 2:313 §8125 and 2:500 §10,507; and Ibn Mājah in *al-Sunan*, 1:71 §197.

Whoever spends a pair in the path of Allah, it will be called out from the doors of Paradise: 'O servant of Allah! This is good.'[1]

3. ᶜAbd Allāh b. ᶜUmar narrates that the Holy Prophet ﷺ said:

لاَ حَسَدَ إِلاَّ عَلَى اثْنَتَيْنِ، رَجُلٌ آتَاهُ اللهُ الْكِتَابَ وَقَامَ بِهِ آنَاءَ اللَّيْلِ، وَرَجُلٌ أَعْطَاهُ اللهُ مَالاً فَهُوَ يَتَصَدَّقُ بِهِ آنَاءَ اللَّيْلِ وَالنَّهَارِ.

There is no envy except for two types of people: a man whom Allah has given the knowledge of the Book and he recites it during the hours of the night; and a man whom Allah has given wealth, and he spends it in charity during the night and the hours of the day.[2]

4. In another narration, ᶜAbd Allāh b. ᶜUmar narrates that the Holy Prophet ﷺ said:

كَفَى بِالْمَرْءِ إِثْمًا أَنْ يَحْبِسَ عَمَّنْ يَمْلِكُ قُوتَهُ.

It is enough for someone to be sinful if he holds back the provision of the one he is in charge of.[3]

5. Abū Mūsā al-Ashᶜarī narrates:

قَالَ النَّبِيُّ ﷺ: عَلَى كُلِّ مُسْلِمٍ صَدَقَةٌ. قَالُوا: فَإِنْ لَمْ يَجِدْ. قَالَ: فَيَعْمَلُ بِيَدَيْهِ فَيَنْفَعُ نَفْسَهُ وَيَتَصَدَّقُ. قَالُوا: فَإِنْ لَمْ يَسْتَطِعْ أَوْ لَمْ

---

[1] Narrated by al-Bukhārī in *al-Ṣaḥīḥ*, 2:671 §1798.

[2] Narrated by al-Bukhārī in *al-Ṣaḥīḥ*, 4:1919 §4737 and 6:2643 §6805; Muslim in *al-Ṣaḥīḥ*, 1:558-559 §815; Aḥmad b. Ḥanbal in *al-Musnad*, 2:8 §4550, 4924, 5618 and 6403; al-Tirmidhī in *al-Jāmiᶜ al-Ṣaḥīḥ*, 4:330 §1936; and Ibn Mājah in *al-Sunan*, 2:408 §4209.

[3] Narrated by Muslim in *al-Ṣaḥīḥ*, 2:692 §996.

يَفْعَلْ. قَالَ: فَيُعِينُ ذَا الْحَاجَةِ الْـمَلْهُوفَ. قَالُوا فَإِنْ لَـمْ يَفْعَلْ قَالَ:
فَيَأْمُرُ بِالْخَيْرِ. أَوْ قَالَ: بِالْـمَعْرُوفِ. قَالَ: فَإِنْ لَـمْ يَفْعَلْ. قَالَ:
فَيُمْسِكُ عَنِ الشَّرِّ، فَإِنَّهُ لَهُ صَدَقَةٌ.

The Prophet ﷺ said, "On every Muslim there is enjoined (a compulsory) charity." They asked, 'If one has nothing?' He said, "He should work with his hands so that he may benefit himself and give in charity." They said, 'If he cannot work or does not work?' He said, "Then he should help the oppressed unhappy person (by word or action or both)." They said, 'If he does not do it?' He said, "Then he should enjoin what is good (or said what is reasonable)." They said, 'If he does not do that'. He said, "Then he should refrain from doing evil, for that will be considered for Him as a charity."[1]

6. ʿĀʾisha al-Ṣiddīqa ﷺ narrates that the Holy Prophet ﷺ said to her:

يَا عَائِشَةُ! لَا تَرُدِّي الْـمِسْكِينَ وَلَوْ بِشِقِّ تَـمْرَةٍ. يَا عَائِشَةُ! أَحِبِّي
الْـمَسَاكِينَ وَقَرِّبِيهِمْ. فَإِنَّ اللهَ يُقَرِّبُكِ يَوْمَ الْقِيَامَةِ.

O ʿĀʾisha! Do not turn away a poor person without giving him something, even if it is only half a date. O ʿĀʾisha! Love the poor and needy and hold them dear to yourself, for Allah will bless you with His nearness.[2]

---

[1] Narrated by al-Bukhārī in *al-Ṣaḥīḥ*, 5:2241 §5676; Muslim in *al-Ṣaḥīḥ*, 2:699 §1008; Aḥmad b. Ḥanbal in *al-Musnad*, 4:395 §19,549; and al-Nasāʾī in *al-Sunan*, 5:64 §2538.
[2] Narrated by al-Tirmidhī in *al-Jāmiʿ al-Ṣaḥīḥ*, 4:577 §2352.

7. Abū Saʿīd al-Khudrī narrates that the Holy Prophet ﷺ said:

أَيُّمَا مُؤْمِنٍ أَطْعَمَ مُؤْمِنًا عَلَى جُوعٍ أَطْعَمَهُ اللهُ يَوْمَ الْقِيَامَةِ مِنْ ثِمَارِ الْجَنَّةِ. وَأَيُّمَا مُؤْمِنٍ سَقَى مُؤْمِنًا عَلَى ظَمَإٍ سَقَاهُ اللهُ يَوْمَ الْقِيَامَةِ مِنَ الرَّحِيقِ الْمَخْتُومِ. وَأَيُّمَا مُؤْمِنٍ كَسَا مُؤْمِنًا عَلَى عُرْيٍ كَسَاهُ اللهُ مِنْ خُضْرِ الْجَنَّةِ.

Whichever believer feeds a hungry believer, Allah feeds him from the fruits of Paradise on the Day of Judgement. Whichever believer gives drink to a thirsty believer, Allah gives him to drink from the 'sealed nectar' on the Day of Judgement. Whichever believer clothes a naked believer, Allah clothes him from the green garments of Paradise.[1]

Q.84. What is *Infāq Wājiba*?

A: *Infāq wājiba* refers to those types of charity that must be paid by those obligated to pay the zakah, such as *ṣadaqa al-fiṭr*, *ʿushr* or any charity which has been pledged in the fulfilment of a vow (*nadhr*).

1. Regarding the obligation of the zakah and its importance, the Qurʾān has given explicit commandments in many places. For example in *Sūra al-Muzammil*, Allah ﷻ states:

﴿وَأَقِيمُواْ ٱلصَّلَوٰةَ وَءَاتُواْ ٱلزَّكَوٰةَ﴾

[1] Narrated by Abū Dāwūd in *al-Sunan*, 2:130 §1682; and al-Tirmidhī in *al-Jāmiʿ al-Ṣaḥīḥ*, 4:633 §2449.

> *And establish Prayer and pay Zakat (the Alms-due).*[1]

2. In the same way, *ṣadaqa al-fiṭr* is also *wājib* upon every Muslim who has wealth which amount to the *niṣāb*, as it is mentioned in the hadith. ʿAbd Allāh b. ʿUmar narrates:

> أَنَّ رَسُولَ اللهِ ﷺ فَرَضَ زَكَاةَ الْفِطْرِ مِنْ رَمَضَانَ عَلَى كُلِّ نَفْسٍ مِنَ الْـمُسْلِمِينَ حُرٍّ أَوْ عَبْدٍ أَوْ رَجُلٍ أَوِ امْرَأَةٍ صَغِيرٍ أَوْ كَبِيرٍ صَاعًا مِنْ تَمْرٍ أَوْ صَاعًا مِنْ شَعِيرٍ.

> The Messenger of Allah ﷺ prescribed *zakat al-Fiṭr* of *Ramaḍān*, one *ṣāʿ* of dates or one *ṣāʿ* of barley for every individual among the Muslims (whether) free man or slave, male or female, young or old.[2]

The condition of zakah is that one possesses the *niṣāb* after a whole year passes, but in *ṣadaqa al-fiṭr* this condition does not apply. In fact if a person possesses wealth equal to the *niṣāb* on the day of *ʿīd al-fiṭr* and it is in excess of one's basic necessities, he or she will be obligated to pay the *ṣadaqa al-fiṭr*.

3. In the same way any agricultural produce from which *ʿushr* is collected, such as wheat, barley, rice, sugar cane, vegetables, grain, fruit, etc.

ʿAbd Allāh b. ʿUmar narrates that the Holy Prophet ﷺ said:

> فِيمَـا سَقَتِ السَّمَـاءُ وَالْعُيُونُ أَوْ كَانَ عَثَرِيًّا الْعُشْرُ. وَمَا سُقِيَ بِالنَّضْحِ نِصْفُ الْعُشْرِ.

---

[1] Qur'ān 73:20.

[2] Narrated by Muslim in *al-Ṣaḥīḥ*, 2:678 §984.

That land which is irrigated by rain, streams, or is always naturally irrigated, there is (a zakah of) one-tenth (10%); that land which is irrigated by pulling water out of wells, there is (a zakah of) one-twentieth (i.e., 5%).[1]

Q.85. WHAT IS *INFĀQ NĀFILA*?

A: *Infāq nāfila* refers to spending surplus wealth, asset, and property on the poor and needy with the intention of gaining the pleasure of Allah. This spending is in addition to the *infāq wājiba*. The more someone spends, the higher his station is in the hereafter. Allah ﷻ states in the Qur'ān:

﴿مَّثَلُ ٱلَّذِينَ يُنفِقُونَ أَمۡوَٰلَهُمۡ فِي سَبِيلِ ٱللَّهِ كَمَثَلِ حَبَّةٍ أَنۢبَتَتۡ سَبۡعَ سَنَابِلَ فِي كُلِّ سُنۢبُلَةٖ مِّاْئَةُ حَبَّةٖۗ وَٱللَّهُ يُضَٰعِفُ لِمَن يَشَآءُۚ وَٱللَّهُ وَٰسِعٌ عَلِيمٌ﴾

The example of those who spend their wealth in the way of Allah is like (that) grain out of which seven ears shoot forth. (And then) each ear bears a hundred grains (i.e., they are rewarded seven hundred times). And Allah multiplies (still more) for whom He likes. And Allah is Infinite, All-Knowing.[2]

ʿAdī b. Ḥātim narrates that he heard the Holy Prophet ﷺ say:

اِتَّقُوا النَّارَ وَلَوْ بِشِقِّ تَمْرَةٍ.

[1] Narrated by al-Bukhārī in *al-Ṣaḥīḥ*, 2:540 §1412.
[2] Qur'ān 2:261.

> Save yourself from the Hellfire even by half a date.[1]

The Qur'ān has repeatedly encouraged the donation of voluntary charity in addition to the obligatory one.

Q.86. Is there any limit set for the voluntary charity?

A: No, the voluntary charity has no limits; there is no condition of *niṣāb*, nor is a fixed amount to be paid. There is no minimum or maximum amount of charity, but one should take into consideration his own needs and the needs of the poor, on deciding how much he wants to give. The Qur'ān states:

﴿وَيَسْـَٔلُونَكَ مَاذَا يُنفِقُونَ قُلِ ٱلْعَفْوَ﴾

> *And they also ask you about what they should spend. Say: '(Spend) whatever is surplus to your needs.'*[2]

The verses above lay down the principle on spending in the path of Allah that there is no upper limit. One should spare enough money to fulfil his needs and the needs of his family.

Q.87. Which charity requires the *niṣāb*?

A: *Niṣāb* is not required for the *ṣadaqa nāfila*; it is only a requirement in the *ṣadaqa wājiba*. For example, the zakah is a *ṣadaqa wājiba* but it does not become obligatory upon someone who does not meet the *niṣāb*. The amount to be paid in *ṣadaqa wājiba* is also fixed, such as 2.5% for zakah, and 10% or 5% for *ʿushr*.

---

[1] Narrated by al-Bukhārī in *al-Ṣaḥīḥ*, 2:514 §1351.
[2] Qur'ān 2:219.

Q.88. What is the importance of charity in Islam and what warning has been given to those who do not give it?

A: Islam has declared the act of giving in charity as upholding virtue and not giving in charity as rejecting it. This can be proven by the following verses of the Qur'ān which weigh up the affirmation and rejection of virtue. In fact, this comparison begins in a very skilful manner by mentioning the opposites which exist in creation.

Allah ﷻ states:

﴿وَٱلَّيۡلِ إِذَا يَغۡشَىٰ ۝١ وَٱلنَّهَارِ إِذَا تَجَلَّىٰ ۝٢ وَمَا خَلَقَ ٱلذَّكَرَ وَٱلۡأُنثَىٰٓ﴾

By the night when it covers up (and conceals everything in its darkness), and by the day when it brightens up, and by that Being Who created male and female (in everything).[1]

The first two verses mention the contrast between night and day. In the third verse, the division of the human gender into male and female has been mentioned. After categorically mentioning this contrast, it is stated:

﴿إِنَّ سَعۡيَكُمۡ لَشَتَّىٰ﴾

Indeed, your striving is different (and singular).[2]

This verse is stating that some people will certify and uphold virtue by their actions, while others will struggle in rejecting it. However the Qur'ān has categorically decided who is upholding virtue and who is not. Allah ﷻ states:

---

[1] Ibid., 92:1-3.
[2] Ibid., 92:4.

﴿فَأَمَّا مَنْ أَعْطَىٰ وَٱتَّقَىٰ ۝٥ وَصَدَّقَ بِٱلْحُسْنَىٰ ۝٦ فَسَنُيَسِّرُهُۥ لِلْيُسْرَىٰ ۝٧ وَأَمَّا مَنۢ بَخِلَ وَٱسْتَغْنَىٰ ۝٨ وَكَذَّبَ بِٱلْحُسْنَىٰ ۝٩ فَسَنُيَسِّرُهُۥ لِلْعُسْرَىٰ﴾

So he who gives away (his wealth in the way of Allah) and commits himself to piousness, and affirms the good (the Din [Religion]) of truth and life after death through charity and Godwariness), soon We shall facilitate him in seeking (Allah's pleasure) with ease. But he who is miser and disregards (spending in the cause of Allah), and (in this way) denies the good (the Din [Religion]) of truth and afterlife), soon shall We facilitate his landing into hardship (advancing towards torment, so that punishment becomes his rightful due).[1]

Therefore, the Qurʾān in clear terms declares spending in the path of Allah as upholding and certifying virtue; and miserliness has been declared as rejecting it. It has also been made clear that anyone who adopts the practice of spending in the path of Allah, achieving his aims would be made easy for him whereas someone who adopts the path of miserliness and hoarding of wealth, achieving his righteous aims would be made difficult for him. Thus the latter should realise that he is not treading the path of virtue, and that it does not bring him any benefit to his religion, rather it amounts to rejecting it, and whoever rejects the religion is worthy of punishment. The Qurʾān states:

﴿وَمَا يُغْنِي عَنْهُ مَالُهُۥٓ إِذَا تَرَدَّىٰٓ﴾

---

[1] Ibid., 92:5-10.

And his wealth will not help him any way when he falls into (the pit of) destruction.[1]

Q.89. Does spending in the path of Allah serve as a means of purifying the wealth and the inner self?

A: Yes, spending in the path of Allah purifies wealth and the inner self (*nafs*) because it is absolutely clear that the initiation of the goal in gaining the pleasure of Allah is *tazkiyya*; and *tazkiyya* is of two types: purification of the wealth and purification of the inner self. A study of the Qur'ān makes it clear that both types of purification are dependent on *infāq* (spending in the path of Allah) and both are dependent upon each other. The purification gained through the practice of spending in the path of Allah without doubt becomes a cause of purification of the inner self. It will not be out of place to say that the practice of *infāq* is a positive form of the purification of the inner self, i.e., spending in the path of Allah is vital for the purification of the ego.

Allah ﷻ states:

﴿وَسَيُجَنَّبُهَا ٱلْأَتْقَى ﴿١٧﴾ ٱلَّذِى يُؤْتِى مَالَهُۥ يَتَزَكَّىٰ ﴿١٨﴾ وَمَا لِأَحَدٍ عِندَهُۥ
مِن نِّعْمَةٍ تُجْزَىٰٓ ﴿١٩﴾ إِلَّا ٱبْتِغَآءَ وَجْهِ رَبِّهِ ٱلْأَعْلَىٰ ﴿٢٠﴾ وَلَسَوْفَ يَرْضَىٰ﴾

But the most pious one shall be saved from this (Fire), who gives his wealth away (in the cause of Allah) to attain to purity (of his soul and assets), and who owes no favour to anyone that he is seeking to pay back. Rather (he spends) seeking the pleasure of his Lord, Most High. And soon

---

[1] Ibid., 92:11.

shall he be well-pleased (with Allah for His bestowal and Allah with him for his fidelity).[1]

The following principles are derived from the verses quoted above:

1. Spending in the path of Allah is the greatest means of attaining godwariness (*taqwā*).
2. Spending in the path of Allah is a guarantee of ensuring safety from the Hellfire.
3. True *tazkiyya* is gained from spending in the path of Allah.
4. The practice of spending in the path of Allah should only be performed in order to gain the pleasure of Allah.
5. Spending in the path of Allah solely for the pleasure of Allah undoubtedly results in Allah being pleased.

Thus the practice of spending in the path of Allah is not only the means of the purification of wealth, but is also the purification of the inner self because the actual and practical basis of gaining Allah's pleasure is by spending in His path.

Q.90. Is the practice of spending in the path of Allah a means of having one's supplication granted?

A: Yes, the practice of spending in the path of Allah is also a means of one's supplication being accepted. There is a deep relationship between giving charity and having one's supplications granted. Allah ﷻ states:

﴿خُذْ مِنْ أَمْوَٰلِهِمْ صَدَقَةً تُطَهِّرُهُمْ وَتُزَكِّيهِم بِهَا وَصَلِّ عَلَيْهِمْ ۖ إِنَّ
صَلَوٰتَكَ سَكَنٌ لَّهُمْ ۗ وَٱللَّهُ سَمِيعٌ عَلِيمٌ﴾

---

[1] Ibid., 92:17-21.

Collect alms (Zakat—the Alms-due) from their wealth so that by these (alms) you may purify them (of their sins) and (by this purification of faith and riches) bestow upon them blessing and pray for them. Surely, your prayer is a (source of) delightful calm for them. And Allah is All-Hearing, All-Knowing.[1]

Paying attention to the wordings of this verse, the following three points come to the fore:

1. Take charity (i.e., the zakah) from their wealth.
2. Due to this charity, purify them (from sin) and bless them (with the purity of faith and practice).
3. Pray for them, indeed, your supplication for them is a source of comfort for them, and Allah is All-Hearing and All-Knowing.

First of all, there is encouragement and motivation to donate charity stating that this spending in the path of Allah will be the means of removing internal and external impurities. The process of *tazkiyya* which is merely the result of spending in the path of Allah will provide freedom from the darkness of the inner self. Therefore when a person makes the benefit and welfare of creation the ultimate aim of his life then when he supplicates to Allah his prayers will be answered. The realisation of one's prayers provides satisfaction to the heart. Also Allah ﷻ listens to those supplications that you make for your own benefit and he knows of your actions that you do for others.

The more one spends in the path of Allah, the more one's supplications are answered. On the other hand if one ignores the plight of others, violates their rights, is not courteous and caring towards others and limits oneself to the narrow ambit of personal benefit then one's

---

[1] Ibid., 9:103.

supplication will not be accepted. Although supplications never go to waste as they are also a form of worship thus their reward will be received in some way or another, but the desired result of the supplications will not be attained.

Q.91. Can virtuous acts and godwariness be gained without the practice of spending in the path of Allah?

A: Virtue and godwariness (*taqwā*) cannot be gained without spending in the path of Allah. The Qurʾān states:

﴿لَن تَنَالُواْ ٱلْبِرَّ حَتَّىٰ تُنفِقُواْ مِمَّا تُحِبُّونَۚ وَمَا تُنفِقُواْ مِن شَيْءٍ فَإِنَّ ٱللَّهَ بِهِۦ عَلِيمٌ﴾

> *You can never attain to piety unless you spend (in the cause of Allah) out of that which you like the most; and Allah surely knows well whatever you give away.*[1]

Here it has been declared that *birr* (virtue, righteousness and piety) cannot be gained without spending in the path of Allah. There cannot be a clearer and absolute declaration of the Qurʾān that piety and godwariness can only be gained by spending in the path of Allah. So in simpler terms it can be said that *infāq* has been declared to be piety. The principles laid down by this verse on the personal level are that true virtue can only be gained through *infāq*, and without it no action can be declared to be virtuous. True virtue according to Allah can only be gained through the practice of spending in the path of Allah.

---

[1] Ibid., 9:103.

Verse 177 of *Sūra al-Baqara* also supports the reality that true virtue and piety is in spending for the sake of Allah. Allah ﷻ states:

﴿وَلَٰكِنَّ ٱلْبِرَّ مَنْ ءَامَنَ بِٱللَّهِ وَٱلْيَوْمِ ٱلْءَاخِرِ وَٱلْمَلَٰٓئِكَةِ وَٱلْكِتَٰبِ وَٱلنَّبِيِّۦنَ وَءَاتَى ٱلْمَالَ عَلَىٰ حُبِّهِۦ ذَوِى ٱلْقُرْبَىٰ وَٱلْيَتَٰمَىٰ وَٱلْمَسَٰكِينَ وَٱبْنَ ٱلسَّبِيلِ وَٱلسَّآئِلِينَ وَفِى ٱلرِّقَابِ﴾

But true righteousness is that a person believes in Allah, the Last Day, the angels, the Book (revealed by Allah) and the Messengers. Driven by love for Allah, he spends (his) wealth on the kindred, the orphans, the needy, the wayfarers and those who ask and in (liberating slaves') necks.[1]

What is worth noting from this verse is that after fulfilling the condition of faith, the greatest requirement in acquiring piety and godwariness is to spend one's wealth in the path of Allah. Towards the end of this verse Allah ﷻ states:

﴿أُو۟لَٰٓئِكَ ٱلَّذِينَ صَدَقُوا۟ ۖ وَأُو۟لَٰٓئِكَ هُمُ ٱلْمُتَّقُونَ﴾

It is these who are truthful and it is these who are righteous.[2]

Thus, *infāq fī sabīl Allāh* (to spend in the path of Allah) is the first requirement for piety, truthfulness and godwariness.

---

[1] Ibid., 2:177.
[2] Ibid.

Q.92. Which signs have been mentioned of those people who reject the religion in *Sūra al-Māʿūn*?

A: The Qurʾān in *Sūra al-Māʿūn* mentions the following signs of those who reject the religion. Allah ﷻ states:

﴿أَرَءَيْتَ ٱلَّذِى يُكَذِّبُ بِٱلدِّينِ ﴿١﴾ فَذَٰلِكَ ٱلَّذِى يَدُعُّ ٱلْيَتِيمَ ﴿٢﴾ وَلَا
يَحُضُّ عَلَىٰ طَعَامِ ٱلْمِسْكِينِ ﴿٣﴾ فَوَيْلٌ لِّلْمُصَلِّينَ ﴿٤﴾ ٱلَّذِينَ هُمْ عَن
صَلَاتِهِمْ سَاهُونَ ﴿٥﴾ ٱلَّذِينَ هُمْ يُرَآءُونَ ﴿٦﴾ وَيَمْنَعُونَ ٱلْمَاعُونَ﴾

> *Have you seen him who denies the Din (Religion)? So he is the one who pushes away the orphan (i.e., rejects the needs of the orphans and deprives them of their right), and does not promote the cause of feeding the poor (i.e., does not strive to end the economic exploitation of the poor and the needy). So woe to those worshippers, who are unaware of (the spirit of) their Prayers (i.e., they are mindful only of the rights of Allah, but are heedless of the rights of fellow human beings), who show off (their worship, for they only render a formal service to the Creator and are inconsiderate to the oppressed humanity), and who refuse to lend a worthless small object of use even on demand!*[1]

The word '*yatīm*' (orphan) in the second verse of the *sūra* is used in the symbolic sense for all those who are downtrodden in society. This verse points out those who dislike the downtrodden and feel no urge to alleviate their burden.

---

[1] Ibid. 107:1-7.

The word '*yadʿu*' (to push) refers to the fact that orphans are not considered to be equal in status to their self-concocted status in society, and were thus kept far away. They behaved arrogantly with the orphans having no association with them, in fact considering them to be a burden on society. In this verse, the Qur'ān pinpoints a specific mind-set of those people who reject the religion which is found abundantly in some affluent people.

The third verse of the *sūra* mentioned another of their unique features which is that they do not cater for the poor and needy in society, nor do they encourage others to do so. They consider alleviating the downtrodden people out of their economic difficulty not to be important; hence they do not spend in the path of Allah.

Wa lā yaḥuḍḍu notes that their struggle is never aimed at changing the viewpoint of the wealthy in their obligations towards the poor. In this verse, 'encourages' means to bring others to understand through one's speech, actions and efforts that the wealth that they have is not only their own right, but also the right of the poor and needy in society, as the Qur'ān states:

﴿وَفِىٓ أَمْوَٰلِهِمْ حَقٌّ لِّلسَّآئِلِ وَٱلْمَحْرُومِ﴾

> *And in their wealth was appointed a due share for the beggars and the destitute (i.e., all the needy).*[1]

Therefore, those people who on seeing the desperate state of the needy, yet are living their lives carefree without giving a thought to their situation, are the people who reject the religion no matter how religious or pious they consider themselves to be.

---

[1] Ibid., 51:19.

In the following verses, 4-6, by using the term '*muṣallīn*' the Qur'ān has also clarified another point. The act of rejecting the religion can be carried out by those who adhere to the apparent ritual worship. It is possible that some people perform the prayer, yet their behavior is tantamount to rejecting the religion. The Qur'ān is clarifying this matter in very certain terms the destruction and punishment of the hereafter is bound for those people who perform prayer but the spirit of the prayer does not appear in their conduct. The negation of the spirit of the prayer has already been discussed in this *sūra*. By merely praying and considering that the duties of servitude have been met and the requirement of the religion have been fulfilled while at the same time not bothering about the economic miseries of the destitute and needy people in society nor trying to alleviate them from these problem, the Qur'ān makes it clear in certain terms that by doing this the requirement of the religion and the duty of servitude are not fulfilled. Therefore such conduct is considered by Allah to be rejection of the religion. Prayers performed in such a manner only serve the purpose of portraying oneself a worshipper, which will not result in Paradise but being thrown into the Hellfire.

The last sign of those who reject the religion is mentioned in the seventh verse. The rejecters of religion withhold even the least significant of items to themselves. They do not let others take benefit from them. Whereas the concept of *infāq* in Islam also applies to household items in that others have the right to use them. Nobody can own such items in an absolute and unconditional manner that others are not allowed to use them even though they need it. Such conduct has been categorically termed as rejection of the religion.

Q.93. WHAT IS ʿ*ADL*?

A: ʿ*Adl* is when someone is not selfish to the extent that he cares about people in society and is beneficial to them that whatever he likes for himself he at least likes it for others, and if possible he provides them with it. For example, if someone employs a servant, he will provide the servant clothes he would wear himself; and he would feed his servant food which he would eat normally.

Q.94. WHAT IS *IḤSĀN*?

A: *Iḥsān* means beauty, piety and goodness; it comes from the root word *ḥusn*. The antonym of *ḥusn* is *qubḥ* and *sūʾ*, which mean ugliness, evil, and sin. The antonym of *iḥsān* is *isāʾa* which also means ugliness. Imam Abū Manṣūr al-Azharī in *Tahdhīb al-lugha* with regards to the basic meanings of *ḥasana* and *iḥsān*, has quoted al-Layth that Allah ﷻ said:

﴿وَقُولُواْ لِلنَّاسِ حُسْنًا﴾

And (also) talk of piety to the common people (in a polite and pleasant manner).[1]

He says that it means saying something good and nice. In the same way the command to be kind to one's parents has also been given with these words. It is stated in the Qurʾān:

﴿وَوَصَّيْنَا ٱلْإِنسَٰنَ بِوَٰلِدَيْهِ حُسْنًا﴾

And we have enjoined upon man to behave benevolently with his parents.[2]

---

[1] Ibid., 8:83.
[2] Ibid., 29:8.

So while dealing with parents, it must be done in a beautiful and merciful manner. This has been made clear by the word *ḥusnā*. The Qurʾān further clarifies this ruling:

﴿وَلَا تَسْتَوِى ٱلْحَسَنَةُ وَلَا ٱلسَّيِّئَةُ﴾

And good and evil cannot be equal.[1]

So it is clear that good (*ḥasana*) and evil (*sayyiʾa*) can never be equal. The second fundamental point is that evil should not be retaliated by evil, but evil should be countered by good; respond to a bad comment by making a good one. The reason for this being that responding to evil by good words creates an environment of cooperation and love. Evil leads to breakups whilst good leads to agreement; evil leads to hatred while good creates love and unity. This is the reality of *iḥsān*. This is why Allah ﷻ has commanded Muslims to ask for *ḥasana* in this life and the life hereafter.

﴿رَبَّنَآ ءَاتِنَا فِى ٱلدُّنْيَا حَسَنَةً وَفِى ٱلْآخِرَةِ حَسَنَةً وَقِنَا عَذَابَ ٱلنَّارِ﴾

O our Lord, grant us excellence in this world, and excellence in the hereafter (as well), and save us from the torment of the Hell.[2]

It should be noted that in the verse, *ḥasana* does not only refer to pious actions and worship because in the hereafter there will only be reward, not practice. So it is clear that in both cases *ḥasana* refers to *iḥsān*. That is, goodness (*iḥsān*) is being asked for in the world, so that one lives a life full of goodness, free and safe from all

---

[1] Ibid., 41:34.
[2] Ibid., 2:201.

forms of evil, oppression and enmity. In the hereafter, *iḥsān* is being asked for which is a higher status than *ʿadl*. The *ḥasana* in the world refers to all kinds of goodness, and safety from evil and trouble. In the life hereafter, it refers to safety from the punishment, reduction in the severity of the Day of Judgment, ease in the accountability and refuge from the Hellfire.

Two kinds of conduct have been mentioned in the Qurʾān: that is *ʿadl* and *iḥsān*. The Qurʾān states:

﴿إِنَّ ٱللَّهَ يَأۡمُرُ بِٱلۡعَدۡلِ وَٱلۡإِحۡسَٰنِ﴾

Indeed, Allah enjoins justice and benevolence (towards everyone)...[1]

Imam Rāghib al-Aṣfahānī writes that *ʿadl* is that someone pay what is obligatory on him to pay and to receive whatever is his right to receive. However, *iḥsān* is to give more than what is obligatory and to receive less than what one is due; it is to show kindness to others when giving and taking. This is why the rank of *iḥsān* is higher than *ʿadl*. The reward of *ʿadl* is *ʿadl* and the reward of *iḥsān* is *iḥsān*. It is stated in the Qurʾān:

﴿هَلۡ جَزَآءُ ٱلۡإِحۡسَٰنِ إِلَّا ٱلۡإِحۡسَٰنُ﴾

The reward of good cannot be anything but good.[2]

For this reason, it has been decided that when a person gives to others more than is due in the form of *iḥsān*, Allah ﷻ in recompense gives to that person more than what is due to him. It is stated in the Qurʾān:

﴿لِّلَّذِينَ أَحۡسَنُواْ ٱلۡحُسۡنَىٰ وَزِيَادَةٞۖ﴾

---

[1] Ibid., 16:90.
[2] Ibid., 55:60.

For those who do pious works, there is good recompense rather more (added to it).[1]

Those who act upon *iḥsān* will be rewarded with Paradise and then they will be given much more. The exegetes have stated that the word '*ziyāda*' refers to the beatific vision, when the believers will be given the honour of seeing Allah. It is quite interesting that just as Allah ﷻ has given honour and sanctity through Islam, he has mentioned His name *al-Salām*, and just as He gives peace and security through *īmān*, he has mentioned His name *al-Muʾmin*, in the same way Allah ﷻ has given beauty and goodness through *iḥsān*, and He has associated beauty with all His names. The Qurʾān states:

﴿وَلِلَّهِ ٱلْأَسْمَآءُ ٱلْحُسْنَىٰ﴾

And the Most Beautiful Names belong to Allah.[2]

In other words, all Names of Allah (*al-Asmāʾ al-Ḥusnā*) are immensely beautiful. The Qurʾān has commanded *iḥsān* in the fulfillment of all rights due to others. It is stated:

﴿وَأَدَآءٌ إِلَيْهِ بِإِحْسَٰنٍۗ﴾

And (retribution) should be paid (to the heirs of the slain) in a graceful manner.[3]

This is why Allah ﷻ states:

﴿وَإِنَّ ٱللَّهَ لَمَعَ ٱلْمُحْسِنِينَ﴾

And verily Allah blesses the men of spiritual excellence with His companionship.[1]

[1] Ibid., 10:26.
[2] Ibid., 7:180.
[3] Ibid., 2:178.

In this verse, Allah ﷻ has given glad tidings to those who practice *iḥsān* that they will receive His special company. Allah ﷻ also states:

﴿إِنَّ ٱللَّهَ يُحِبُّ ٱلْمُحْسِنِينَ﴾

Verily, Allah loves the righteous.[2]

Those who practice *iḥsān* have been informed of their reward that Allah ﷻ loves them. In another verse, Allah ﷻ states:

﴿مَا عَلَى ٱلْمُحْسِنِينَ مِن سَبِيلٍ﴾

No way can the righteous (i.e., the spirituality excellent) be blamed.[3]

Allah ﷻ has blessed those who practice *iḥsān* with special divine protection. In another place the Qurʾān states:

﴿وَمَنْ أَحْسَنُ دِينًا مِّمَّنْ أَسْلَمَ وَجْهَهُۥ لِلَّهِ وَهُوَ مُحْسِنٌ﴾

And with regards to adopting the Dīn (Religion), who can be better than the one who submits his whole being entirely to Allah, whilst he also holds spiritual excellence.[4]

Allah ﷻ has prescribed *iḥsān* as means of protection from destruction:

﴿وَأَنفِقُوا۟ فِى سَبِيلِ ٱللَّهِ وَلَا تُلْقُوا۟ بِأَيْدِيكُمْ إِلَى ٱلتَّهْلُكَةِ وَأَحْسِنُوٓا۟ إِنَّ ٱللَّهَ يُحِبُّ ٱلْمُحْسِنِينَ﴾

---

[1] Ibid., 29:69.
[2] Ibid., 2:195.
[3] Ibid., 9:91.
[4] Ibid., 4:125.

And spend in the cause of Allah; and do not cast yourselves into destruction with your own hands; and adopt righteousness. Verily, Allah loves the righteous.[1]

This is why every individual is obligated to include *iḥsān* in his every action. This is why killing has been prohibited, and even while slaughtering an animal given undue pain and distress to the animal is also prohibited.

1. In the narration of *Ṣaḥīḥ Muslim* and other books, Shaddād b. Aws narrates that the Holy Prophet ﷺ said:

إِنَّ اللهَ كَتَبَ الإِحْسَانَ عَلَى كُلِّ شَيْءٍ فَإِذَا قَتَلْتُمْ فَأَحْسِنُوا الْقِتْلَةَ وَإِذَا ذَبَحْتُمْ فَأَحْسِنُوا الذَّبْحَ وَلْيُحِدَّ أَحَدُكُمْ شَفْرَتَهُ فَلْيُرِحْ ذَبِيحَتَهُ.

Verily Allah ﷻ has enjoined excellence in everything; so when you kill, kill in an excellent way and when you slaughter, slaughter in an excellent way. So every one of you should sharpen his knife, and let the slaughtered animal die comfortably.[2]

2. Abū Shurayḥ al-Khuzzāʿī narrates that the Holy Prophet ﷺ said:

مَنْ كَانَ يُؤْمِنُ بِاللهِ وَالْيَوْمِ الْآخِرِ فَلْيُحْسِنْ إِلَى جَارِهِ.

Whoever believes in Allah and the Last Day let him treat his neighbour with excellence.[3]

3. Abū Dharr narrates that the Holy Prophet ﷺ said:

---

[1] Ibid., 2:195.
[2] Narrated by Muslim in *al-Ṣaḥīḥ*, 3:1548 §1955.
[3] Ibid., 1:69 §48.

اِتَّقِ اللهَ حَيْثُمَا كُنْتَ، وَأَتْبِعِ السَّيِّئَةَ الْحَسَنَةَ تَمْحُهَا، وَخَالِقِ النَّاسِ بِخُلُقٍ حَسَنٍ.

> Fear Allah wherever you are. And follow up a bad deed with a good deed in order to wipe it out; and behave with people with good conduct.[1]

Q.95. WHAT IS THE DIFFERENCE BETWEEN ʿ*ADL* AND *IḤSĀN*?

A: In general terms, *iḥsān* is treating others well. Its proper meaning is clarified in this verse:

﴿إِنَّ ٱللَّهَ يَأْمُرُ بِٱلْعَدْلِ وَٱلْإِحْسَٰنِ وَإِيتَآيِٕ ذِى ٱلْقُرْبَىٰ وَيَنْهَىٰ عَنِ ٱلْفَحْشَآءِ وَٱلْمُنكَرِ وَٱلْبَغْىِ ۚ يَعِظُكُمْ لَعَلَّكُمْ تَذَكَّرُونَ﴾

> *Indeed, Allah enjoins justice and benevolence (towards everyone), and giving away to the kindred, and forbids indecency, evil deeds, defiance and disobedience. He admonishes you so that you may remember with concern.*[2]

In this verse, two things have been discussed:

1. ʿ*Adl* (equity)
2. *Iḥsān* (benevolence)

The difference between the two has been described by Imam Rāghib al-Aṣfahānī:

> ʿ*Adl* is to give what is obligatory to give and to take what is one's right to take. Whereas *iḥsān* is to give more than what is obligatory and to receive less than what one is due.[3]

---

[1] Narrated by al-Tirmidhī in *al-Jāmiʿ al-Ṣaḥīḥ*, 4:355 §1987.
[2] Qurʾān 16:90.
[3] Rāghib al-Aṣfahānī, *al-Mufradāt*, p. 325.

With regards to this, Shaykh-ul-Islam Dr. Muhammad Tahir-ul-Qadri writes in his book, the 'Islamic Philosophy of Life', that the above mentioned standard for *ᶜadl* and *iḥsān* is based on the minimum level because it is being ordered, and an order is based on something that is compulsory to carry out; failure to do so is a sin. If there is no minimum level of *ᶜadl* and *iḥsān* then one will be sinful. Therefore this meaning of *iḥsān* which is at the level of *farḍ* is interpreted as 'just *ihsan*', whilst the 'perfect *iḥsān*' is for someone to sacrifice all their rights for others.

ᶜAdl is to benefit oneself and also to let others benefit.

Iḥsān is to sacrifice one's right and to bestow it to others.

ᶜAdl is to live for oneself and also live for others.

Iḥsān is to only live for the sake of others.

ᶜAdl is not to trouble others.

Iḥsān is to share others in one's joys.

ᶜAdl is a condition of *īmān*.

Iḥsān is the perfection of *īmān*.

The following hadith narrated by ᶜUmar b. al-Khaṭṭāb also gives a comparative analysis of *ᶜadl* and *iḥsān*:

أَمَرَنَا رَسُولُ ا ﷺ أَنْ نَتَصَدَّقَ فَوَافَقَ ذَلِكَ عِنْدِي مَالاً فَقُلْتُ: الْيَوْمَ أَسْبِقُ أَبَا بَكْرٍ إِنْ سَبَقْتُهُ يَوْمًا. قَالَ: فَجِئْتُ بِنِصْفِ مَالِي. فَقَالَ رَسُولُ ا ﷺ: مَا أَبْقَيْتَ لأَهْلِكَ. قُلْتُ: مِثْلَهُ. وَأَتَى أَبُو بَكْرٍ بِكُلِّ مَا عِنْدَهُ فَقَالَ: يَا أَبَا بَكْرٍ مَا أَبْقَيْتَ لأَهْلِكَ. قَالَ: أَبْقَيْتُ لَهُمُ اللهَ وَرَسُولَهُ. قُلْتُ وَاللهِ لاَ أَسْبِقُهُ إِلَى شَيْءٍ أَبَدًا.

We were ordered by the Messenger of Allah ﷺ to give in charity, and that coincided with a time in which I had some wealth, so I said, "Today I will beat Abū Bakr, if ever I beat him." So I came

> with half of my wealth, and the Messenger of Allah ﷺ said: "What did you leave for your family?" I said: "The like of it." And Abū Bakr came with everything he had, so he said: "O Abū Bakr! What did you leave for your family?" He said: "I left Allah and His Messenger for them." I said: "By Allah, I will never be able to beat him to something."[1]

This hadith makes it clear that the practice of ᶜUmar al-Fārūq ؓ reflected *ᶜadl* whereas the practice of Abū Bakr al-Ṣiddīq ؓ mirrored *iḥsān*.

Q.96. How many ways are there to spend in the path of Allah?

A: There are two ways of spending in the path of Allah: the individual method and the collective method.

I. The Individual Method

The individual method of spending in the path of Allah is to cater for those individuals who are within one's circle of concern; those who are facing economic difficulties and are deprived of basic needs rendering them to be an economically dormant part of society. They should be assisted in such a way that their self-respect is not tainted. The purpose is to prevent such people from being reliant upon others so that their economic deadlock is removed and that they play a positive role in society as respectable citizens. This enabling allows them to gain their deserved status in society. In this regard, other than close relatives and neighbours those people who are more deserving are those who have devoted their lives in the service of Islam in such a way that they have no time to earn a living.

[1] Narrated by al-Tirmidhī in *al-Jāmiᶜ al-Ṣaḥīḥ*, 6:614 §3675.

They are so involved in the service of Islam that they have no concern with their living, business or affairs. If these people became economically inactive then the service to the religion and the work and struggle in reviving the *Umma* will be suspended.

Allah ﷻ states in the Qurʾān:

﴿لِلْفُقَرَآءِ ٱلَّذِينَ أُحْصِرُوا۟ فِى سَبِيلِ ٱللَّهِ لَا يَسْتَطِيعُونَ ضَرْبًا فِى ٱلْأَرْضِ يَحْسَبُهُمُ ٱلْجَاهِلُ أَغْنِيَآءَ مِنَ ٱلتَّعَفُّفِ تَعْرِفُهُم بِسِيمَٰهُمْ لَا يَسْـَٔلُونَ ٱلنَّاسَ إِلْحَافًا ۗ وَمَا تُنفِقُوا۟ مِنْ خَيْرٍ فَإِنَّ ٱللَّهَ بِهِۦ عَلِيمٌ ۝٢٧٣ ٱلَّذِينَ يُنفِقُونَ أَمْوَٰلَهُم بِٱلَّيْلِ وَٱلنَّهَارِ سِرًّا وَعَلَانِيَةً فَلَهُمْ أَجْرُهُمْ عِندَ رَبِّهِمْ وَلَا خَوْفٌ عَلَيْهِمْ وَلَا هُمْ يَحْزَنُونَ﴾

(Charity is) the right of those poor who have been restricted (from earning their livelihood) in the cause of Allah. They cannot even move about in the land (due to their whole time involvement in matters of Din [Religion]). Because of their (ascetic) aversion to greed, the unwise (knowing little about their state of heart and soul) consider them wealthy. You will recognize them from their appearance. They do not ask people (for help) at all lest they should humble themselves (before them). And whatever wealth you give in charity, Allah indeed knows it well. Those who spend (in the cause of Allah) by night and day, privately or publicly, have their reward with their Lord. And (on the Day of Resurrection) they shall neither fear nor grieve.[1]

---

[1] Qurʾān 2:273-274.

II. THE COLLECTIVE METHOD

The collective method of spending in the path of Allah refers to setting up a system that leaves no individual within society needy or in economic inactivity. In this way the society which is set up will be economically stable enabling it to play its effective role in achieving their national vision. It is important to note that in order to achieve the national vision the plan of action must come about by the three main departments that is political, economic and social being inter-connected. This vision is to revive the religion in order to bring about a model society at the global level whose aim is to get rid of oppression, suppression, economic injustice and social evils at every level. So collective spending can only develop when there is re-ordering at the political, economic, and social level; such a model society can be brought about which uproots all kinds of oppression and exploitation.

The Islamic economic system has a perfect solution in order to alleviate the poverty of needy people: poverty is alleviated through the affluent playing their role in society as ordained by the Shariah. The Qur'ān states:

﴿وَٱلَّذِينَ فِيٓ أَمۡوَٰلِهِمۡ حَقّٞ مَّعۡلُومٞ ٢٤ لِّلسَّآئِلِ وَٱلۡمَحۡرُومِ﴾

And those (who are committed to sacrifice and) in whose wealth there is a fixed share, of one who begs and of one who is needy but does not beg.[1]

﴿وَفِيٓ أَمۡوَٰلِهِمۡ حَقّٞ لِّلسَّآئِلِ وَٱلۡمَحۡرُومِ﴾

---

[1] Ibid., 70:24-25.

And in their wealth was appointed a due share for the beggars and the destitute (i.e., all the needy).[1]

Another form of spending at the collective level is that the government takes money from the treasury (*bayt al-māl*) and distributes it amongst the poor. ʿUmar ﷺ had specified quotas for the poor and destitute which he used to take from the treasury. Abū ʿUbayd al-Qāsim b. Salām states:

فَكَانَ عُمَرُ يُعْطِي كُلَّ إِنْسَانٍ مِنْهُمْ كُلَّ سَنَةٍ ثَلاثَةَ آلافٍ.

ʿUmar used to give every person from them [the poor] three thousand (3000) each year.[2]

This is a great example of spending at the collective level. Therefore every country should have an ongoing process of collective and individual spending in order to improve its economic situation.

Q.97. What are the economic benefits of spending in the path of Allah?

A: Whereas spending in the path of Allah bestows one nearness to Allah, the will to sacrifice, godwariness, purity, blessings, longer life and safety from calamities, it also has immeasurable economic benefits. Some economic benefits of spending are given below:

1. The gap between the rich and poor is reduced.
2. The tension between the rich and poor is diminished.
3. The one who spends in the path of Allah seeking Allah's pleasure is not classed as being exorbitant.
4. There is a balanced and systematic distribution of wealth.

---

[1] Ibid., 51:19.

[2] Abū ʿUbayd, *Kitāb al-amwāl*, p. 310 §609.

5. Hoarding commodities of daily use and avoiding paying the zakah is discouraged.
6. There is a reduction of unemployment.
7. Arrangements are made to care for the needy.
8. Begging, being a burden on others and reluctance to earn a living is discouraged.
9. The circulation of wealth in the economy increases the number of products and services and thus leads to increase in trade. This in turn makes economic prosperity in society more certain.
10. When the needy and economically exploited are provided employment, there are not only positive economic results but many of the social ills such as theft, robbery, jealousy, envy and murder are eliminated, and the country sets out on the path of economic development and prosperity.

Q.98. IN LIGHT OF THE HOLY PROPHET'S LIFE, WHAT IS THE PERFECT MODEL OF SPENDING IN THE PATH OF ALLAH?

A: The Holy Prophet ﷺ is the perfect model of spending in the path of Allah. He would spend everything for the sake of Allah's pleasure. If we study the biography of the Holy Prophet ﷺ we would clearly see what status spending in the path of Allah had in the Prophet's life. The Holy Prophet ﷺ used to distribute whatever he had to the poor, needy and those who asked for help. He would undergo poverty and hunger to alleviate the poverty of others. If the Holy Prophet ﷺ had only one morsel to eat and there was a needy person, he would give it to that person. By helping the needy the Holy Prophet ﷺ set such a great example of spending the path of Allah the likes of which cannot be found in the whole of humanity till the end of time.

1. Jābir b. ʿAbd Allāh narrates:

مَا سُئِلَ رَسُولُ ا ﷺ شَيْئًا قَطُّ، فَقَالَ: لَا.

The Messenger of Allah ﷺ was never asked for something ever and he said, 'no'.[1]

2. Anas b. Mālik narrates:

أَنَّ رَجُلاً سَأَلَ النَّبِيَّ ﷺ غَنَمًا بَيْنَ جَبَلَيْنِ فَأَعْطَاهُ إِيَّاهُ فَأَتَى قَوْمَهُ فَقَالَ أَيْ قَوْمِ أَسْلِمُوا فَوَاللهِ إِنَّ مُحَمَّدًا لَيُعْطِي عَطَاءً مَا يَخَافُ الْفَقْرَ.

A man asked the Holy Prophet ﷺ to given him a very large flock between two mountains and he gave it to him. He returned to his tribe and said: 'O my people! Enter into Islam, for by God Muhammad gives so much he does not fear poverty.'

Anas stated that the person entered into Islam for no other reason except for the world, but after he became a Muslim Islam became dearer to him than the world and all that it contains.[2]

3. ʿAbd Allāh b. ʿAbbās narrates that the Holy Prophet ﷺ was the most benevolent of people. When Angel Jibrīl ﷺ would meet him in the month of *Ramaḍān*, the Holy Prophet ﷺ used to show much more generosity. At the time of meeting Angel Jibrīl ﷺ, the Prophet's generosity would be more than a fast wind (which causes rain and welfare).[3]

4. Abū Hurayra narrates that the Holy Prophet ﷺ said:

---

[1] Narrated by Muslim in *al-Ṣaḥīḥ*, 4:1805 §2311.

[2] Ibid., 4:1806 §2312; and al-Bayhaqī in *al-Sunan al-kubrā*, 7:19 §12,967.

[3] Narrated by al-Bukhārī in *al-Ṣaḥīḥ*, 2:672 §1803.

لَوْ كَانَ لِي مِثْلُ أُحُدٍ ذَهَبًا، لَسَرَّنِي أَنْ لَا تَمُرَّ عَلَيَّ ثَلَاثُ لَيَالٍ وَعِنْدِي مِنْهُ شَيْءٌ إِلَّا شَيْئًا أَرْصُدُهُ لِدَيْنٍ.

If I had gold equal to Mount *Uḥud*, it would be pleasing to me that three nights would not pass except that I would not have anything left of it (i.e. I will distribute it all in the path of Allah); except that I would keep some of it to repay debts.[1]

5. The Holy Prophet ﷺ was so generous that he did not even leave anything for himself or his family. Anas b. Mālik narrates:

أَنَّهُ مَشَى إِلَى النَّبِيِّ ﷺ بِخُبْزِ شَعِيرٍ، وَإِهَالَةٍ سَنِخَةٍ، وَلَقَدْ رَهَنَ النَّبِيُّ ﷺ دِرْعًا لَهُ بِالْمَدِينَةِ عِنْدَ يَهُودِيٍّ، وَأَخَذَ مِنْهُ شَعِيرًا لِأَهْلِهِ، وَلَقَدْ سَمِعْتُهُ يَقُولُ: مَا أَمْسَى عِنْدَ آلِ مُحَ ﷺ صَاعُ بُرٍّ وَلاَ صَاعُ حَبٍّ، وَإِنَّ عِنْدَهُ لَتِسْعَ نِسْوَةٍ.

He went to the Prophet ﷺ with barley bread having some dissolved fat on it. The Prophet ﷺ had mortgaged his armour to a Jew in Medina and took from him some barley for his family. Anas heard him saying, "The household of Muhammad did not possess even a single *ṣāʿ* of wheat or food grains for the evening meal, although he has nine wives to look after."[2]

6. ʿĀʾisha al-Ṣiddīqa ؓ narrates:

---

[1] Ibid., 5:2368 §6080; Muslim in *al-Ṣaḥīḥ*, 2:687 §991; and Aḥmad b. Ḥanbal in *al-Musnad*, 2:349 §8579.
[2] Ibid., 2:729 §1963.

مَا شَبِعَ آلُ مُحَمَّدٍ مُنْذُ قَدِمَ الْمَدِينَةَ مِنْ طَعَامِ الْبُرِّ ثَلَاثَ لَيَالٍ تِبَاعًا حَتَّى قُبِضَ.

The family of Muhammad ﷺ never ate (a loaf of) wheat for three consecutive days since their arrival in Medina, until the day he passed away.[1]

Q.99. What is the perfect model of spending in the path of Allah in light of the example of the *Ahl al-bayt*?

A: The *Ahl al-bayt* (the family of the Holy Prophet), following the Prophetic example used to spend all their wealth and income on others whilst their own home mirrored poverty and hunger. After the Holy Prophet ﷺ, no one could match the spending in the path of Allah, *iḥsān* and the adoption of poverty of that of the family of the Holy Prophet ﷺ.

1. ʿĀʾisha al-Ṣiddīqa ﵂ narrates:

إِنْ كُنَّا آلَ مُحَمَّدٍ لَنَمْكُثُ شَهْرًا مَا نَسْتَوْقِدُ بِنَارٍ، إِنْ هُوَ إِلَّا التَّمْرُ وَالْمَاءُ.

We the family of Muhammad ﷺ used to spend (the whole) month in which we did not kindle fire (as we had nothing to cook); we only had dates and water.[2]

2. ʿUrwa b. Zubayr states that it was the habit of ʿĀʾisha al-Ṣiddīqa ﵂ that whenever any of Allah's

[1] Ibid., 5:2067 §5100; Muslim in *al-Ṣaḥīḥ*, 4:2281-2282 §2970; and Aḥmad b. Ḥanbal in *al-Musnad*, 6:46 §24,197.

[2] Narrated by Muslim in *al-Ṣaḥīḥ*, 4:2282 §2970; al-Tirmidhī in *al-Jāmiʿ al-Ṣaḥīḥ*, 4:645 §2471; and Ibn Mājah in *al-Sunan*, 2:1388 §4144.

provision would come to her she would not keep it with her; instead she would donate it (there and then).

ʿUrwa further states that once ten slaves were sent to her, but she freed them straight away. Even when forty slaves were sent to her she freed them.[1]

3. ʿAbd Allāh b. Zubayr states that he never saw any female more generous than ʿĀʾisha and Asmāʾ. The difference between them was that ʿĀʾisha used to collect things and then distribute them, whilst her sister Asmāʾ did not used to keep things with her, but would distribute them straight away.[2]

4. Mother of the believers, ʿĀʾisha ﵂, narrates:

قَالَ رَسُولُ ا ﷺ: أَسْرَعُكُنَّ لَحَاقًا بِي أَطْوَلُكُنَّ يَدًا. قَالَتْ فَكُنَّ يَتَطَاوَلْنَ أَيَّتُهُنَّ أَطْوَلُ يَدًا. قَالَتْ: فَكَانَتْ أَطْوَلَنَا يَدًا زَيْنَبُ لأَنَّهَا كَانَتْ تَعْمَلُ بِيَدِهَا وَتَصَدَّقُ.

> Allah's Messenger ﷺ said: "One who has the longest hands amongst you would meet me most immediately." She farther said: They (the wives of Allah's Messenger) used to measure the hands as to whose hand was the longest and it was the hand of Zaynab that was the longest amongst them, as she used to work with her hand and spend (that income) on charity.[3]

The same narration is found in *Ṣaḥīḥ al-Bukhārī* with the following words. ʿĀʾisha ﵂ narrates:

[1] Narrated by al-Bukhārī in *al-Ṣaḥīḥ*, 3:1291 §3314.
[2] Narrated by al-Bukhārī in *al-Adab al-mufrad*, p.106 §280.
[3] Narrated by Muslim in *al-Ṣaḥīḥ*, 4:1907 §2452.

أَنَّ بَعْضَ أَزْوَاجِ النَّبِيِّ قُلْنَ لِلنَّبِيِّ ﷺ: أَيُّنَا أَسْرَعُ بِكَ لُحُوقًا. قَالَ: أَطْوَلُكُنَّ يَدًا. فَأَخَذُوا قَصَبَةً يَذْرَعُونَهَا، فَكَانَتْ سَوْدَةُ أَطْوَلَهُنَّ يَدًا، فَعَلِمْنَا بَعْدُ أَنَّمَا كَانَتْ طُولَ يَدِهَا الصَّدَقَةُ، وَكَانَتْ أَسْرَعَنَا لُحُوقًا بِهِ وَكَانَتْ تُحِبُّ الصَّدَقَةَ.

Some of the wives of the Prophet ﷺ asked him, "Who amongst us will be the first to follow you (i.e. die after you)?" He said, "Whoever has the longest hand." So they started measuring their hands with a stick and Sawda's hand turned out to be the longest. (When Zaynab bint Jaḥsh died first of all in the caliphate of ʿUmar), we came to know that the long hand was a symbol of practicing charity, so she was the first to follow the Prophet ﷺ and she used to love to practice charity. (Sawda died later in the caliphate of Muʿāwiya).[1]

5. It is narrated that Imam Ḥasan and Ḥusayn ‎ became ill, so Sayyidunā ʿAlī, Sayyida Fāṭima, and their servant Fiḍa ‎ vowed to fast three days for the return of their health. Allah ‎ blessed them with good health, so in order to fulfil their vows they fasted. ʿAlī ‎ bought three *ṣāʿ* of wheat and Sayyida Fāṭima ‎ would make bread with one *ṣāʿ* each day. However, when it was time for breaking the fast, the food was in front of them ready to be eaten when a destitute came to the door asking for food. Seeking Allah's pleasure they gave the loaf of bread to the destitute and instead had water to break their fast.

[1] Narrated by al-Bukhārī in *al-Ṣaḥīḥ*, 2:515 §1354.

On the second and third day, the same thing happened when an orphan and prisoner came respectively.[1]

Fasting in this way for three days was such a model of sacrifice that it was mentioned in the Qurʾān:

﴿يُوفُونَ بِٱلنَّذۡرِ وَيَخَافُونَ يَوۡمٗا كَانَ شَرُّهُۥ مُسۡتَطِيرٗا ٧ وَيُطۡعِمُونَ
ٱلطَّعَامَ عَلَىٰ حُبِّهِۦ مِسۡكِينٗا وَيَتِيمٗا وَأَسِيرًا ٨ إِنَّمَا نُطۡعِمُكُمۡ لِوَجۡهِ
ٱللَّهِ لَا نُرِيدُ مِنكُمۡ جَزَآءٗ وَلَا شُكُورًا ٩ إِنَّا نَخَافُ مِن رَّبِّنَا يَوۡمًا
عَبُوسٗا قَمۡطَرِيرٗا﴾

(These privileged servants of Allah are those) who fulfil their vows and keep fearing that Day whose severity spreads afar. And they give (their own) food, in deep love of Allah, to the needy, the orphan and prisoner (out of sacrifice, despite their own desire and need for it), (and say:) 'We are feeding you only to please Allah. We do not seek any recompense from you nor (wish for) any thanks. We fear from our Lord the Day which will make (the faces) look very dark (and) ugly.'[2]

6. Such was the model of sacrifice of Mawlā ʿAlī عليه السلام that he used to give away so much in charity that throughout his life he never reached the *niṣāb*.

7. Charity and benevolence towards one's family was an attribute of Imam Ḥasan. Not only was he benevolent, he used to be pleased with the benevolence of others. One day on passing an orchard he saw an Abyssinian slave eating bread; whilst he was eating bread, he would take one morsel for himself and give another to the dog. In this

---

[1] Al-Thaʿlabī, *al-Kashf wa al-bayān*, 10:98-101; al-Baghawī, *Maʿālim al-Tanzīl*, 4:428; and al-Qurṭubī, *al-Jāmiʿ li aḥkām al-Qurʾān*, 19:131.

[2] Qurʾān 76:7-10.

way he fed half of the bread to the dog. Imam Ḥasan asked the slave, 'Why did you not drive the dog away'. He replied, 'I felt a veil between my eyes and his eyes.' Imam Ḥasan asked, 'Who are you?' He replied, 'The slave of Ābān b. ʿUthmān.' Imam Ḥasan said to the slave, 'Do not go anywhere until I return.' Right away Imam Ḥasan went to Ābān and bought both the orchard and the slave. When Imam Ḥasan returned he said to the slave, 'I have bought you.' He stood up in respect and said, 'My master! I am here to serve Allah and His Messenger, so whatever you command.' Imam Ḥasan told him that he bought him and has set him free and has gifted the orchard to him for the sake of Allah. The slave replied, 'The path of whom you have freed me, I donate this orchard in His path.'[1]

8. It is narrated that once Imam Ḥasan gathered a large sum for the poor and needy. Sayyidunā ʿAlī announced its distribution. People thought that this distribution was for all, so a large number of people began to assemble. Seeing this flood of people, Imam Ḥasan announced that this money is only for the poor and needy. Upon this announcement, about half of the people remained. The first to get a share was Ashʿath b. Qays.[2]

9. Imam Ḥusayn ﵇ showed such benevolence and spending in the path of Allah that it reflected the great wealth that Allah ﷻ had blessed him. Ibn ʿAsākir writes that Imam Ḥusayn ﵇ used to give charity in the path of Allah. No needy person returned empty from his door. Once a poor person came to his home, but the Imam at that time was engaged in the ritual prayer. On hearing the call of the wonderer he quickly finished his prayer and came out. The wonderer showed the effects of hunger and being destitute. He called his servant straight away and asked, 'Is there anything left from our expenditure?' The

---

[1] Ibn ʿAsākir, *Tārīkh Dimashq al-kabīr*, 13:246.
[2] Ibid.

servant replied, 'You gave me two hundred (200) dirhams to distribute amongst the *ahl al-bayt*, which has not been distributed yet.' The Imam said, "Bring that money because this man is more deserving than the *ahl al-bayt*." Then on receiving the bag of two hundred (200) dirhams he gave it to the man and apologised for it being so little because that was all he had at the time.[1]

The additional quality of this practice of the *ahl al-bayt* is that they did not demand being thanked in any way for their sacrifices but only considered such practice to be necessary for the betterment of their life hereafter. The reality is that only spending in the path of Allah that is carried out with this level of benevolence (*iḥsān*) can be considered to be a model of perfection and a standard.

Q.100. What is the model of perfection of spending in the path of Allah in the light of the examples of the Companions?

A: The Companions are those great people who directly benefitted from the blessings of Prophethood and who lived their lives in following the great example of the Holy Prophet ﷺ. This is why they also rank as exemplars for the *Umma*. Declaring the lives of the Companions models, the Qur'ān states:

﴿وَٱلَّذِينَ تَبَوَّءُو ٱلدَّارَ وَٱلْإِيمَٰنَ مِن قَبْلِهِمْ يُحِبُّونَ مَنْ هَاجَرَ إِلَيْهِمْ وَلَا يَجِدُونَ فِى صُدُورِهِمْ حَاجَةً مِّمَّآ أُوتُوا۟ وَيُؤْثِرُونَ عَلَىٰٓ أَنفُسِهِمْ وَلَوْ كَانَ بِهِمْ خَصَاصَةٌ ۚ وَمَن يُوقَ شُحَّ نَفْسِهِۦ فَأُو۟لَٰٓئِكَ هُمُ ٱلْمُفْلِحُونَ﴾

(These spoils are for those Ansar [Supporters] as well) who had taken the city (of Medina) and the

[1] Qur'ān 14:158.

> *faith as their home before (the Emigrants came). They love those who have come to them as Emigrants, and do not feel any need (or niggardly feeling) in their hearts pertaining to that (wealth) which is given to the Emigrants, and prefer them to themselves, even though they may themselves be in dire need. And he who is saved from the miserliness of his (ill-commanding) self, it is they who are successful and victorious.*[1]

The perfect model of spending in the path of Allah in light of the biography of the Companions is that they gave preference to spend in charity than to fulfill their own personal needs and adopted the practice of spending in the path of Allah and sacrificing as much as possible. The hadiths and the books of history support the fact that the practical example of sacrifice and spending in the path of Allah that was shown by Abū Bakr al-Ṣiddīq ﵁ after embracing Islam is unique.

Hishām narrates from his father:

> The day Abū Bakr embraced Islam he owned forty thousand (40,000) dinars (gold coins) at that time. He spent all his wealth in the path of Allah.[2]

It appears that embracing Islam established intense love for the mission of the Holy Prophet ﷺ that he saw it as the only worthy cause to spend all his wealth.

ᶜUmar b. al-Khaṭṭāb al-Fārūq ﵁ was also an exemplar of sacrifice and benevolence. Zayd b. Aslam narrates from his father that ᶜAbd Allāh b. ᶜUmar asked him about some matters concerning ᶜUmar. He said that since the Holy Prophet ﷺ passed away, he did not see anyone more

---

[1] Ibid., 59:9.
[2] Ibn ᶜAsākir, *Tārīkh Dimashq al-kabīr*, 30:67.

serious, hardworking and generous than ʿUmar b. al-Khaṭṭāb.[1]

His practice of benevolence and altruism continued in the same way after becoming the caliph. The following statement of this is clear evidence of this:

لَوْ مَاتَتْ شَاةٌ عَلَى شَاطِئِ الْفُرَاتِ ضَائِعَةً لَظَنَنْتُ أَنَّ اللهَ سَائِلِي عَنْهَا يَوْمَ الْقِيَامَةِ.

> If a sheep gets lost and dies on the banks of the Euphrates River, I fear that Allah will question me about it on the Day of Judgement.[2]

He has the same endeavour of spending in the path of Allah and sacrificing that was given to all Companions and the *ahl al-bayt* from the perfect model of the Holy Prophet ﷺ. These attributes were not confined to him alone but his family also mirrored them. This can be judged by the practice of his son, ʿAbd Allāh b. ʿUmar. Nāfiʿ narrates:

كَانَ ابْنُ عُمَرَ لَا يَأْكُلُ حَتَّى يُؤْتَى بِمِسْكِينٍ يَأْكُلُ مَعَهُ.

> Ibn ʿUmar never used to eat until he brought a poor person to eat with him.[3]

The manner in which ʿUthmān b. ʿAffān lived his life in not hidden from anyone. After the migration to Medina, he bought a well for the Muslims, and he bought land for the Prophet's Mosque. He used to pay for the equipment of the infantry and free many slaves. He spent plenty of his wealth in improving the economic situation of the Companions. At a time of famine and scarcity, he

---

[1] Narrated by al-Bukhārī in *al-Ṣaḥīḥ*, 3:1348 §3484.
[2] Ibn Jawzī, *Manāqib ʿUmar b. al-Khaṭṭāb*, p.161.
[3] Narrated by al-Bukhārī in *al-Ṣaḥīḥ*, 5:2061 §5078.

imported wheat and distributed it amongst the people of Medina free of charge. In following every instruction of the Holy Prophet ﷺ, he set such example of *iḥsān* that it remains a standard for humanity forever.

ʿAbd al-Raḥmān b. Khabbāb states: I came to the Holy Prophet ﷺ when he was motivating people regarding *jaysh ʿusra*. ʿUthmān b. ʿAffān stood up and said, 'O Messenger of Allah! I take the responsibility of one hundred camels including all equipment for them.' The Holy Prophet ﷺ then again motivated the people and ʿUthmān b. ʿAffān stood up again and said, 'O Messenger of Allah! I take up the responsibility of providing two hundred (200) camels together with their equipment and grain.' The Holy Prophet ﷺ again motivated the people so ʿUthmān stood up for a third time and said, 'I accept the responsibility for three hundred (300) camels including all their equipment.' The narrator states that the Holy Prophet ﷺ came down from the pulpit and prayed to Allah not to hold ʿUthmān responsible for whatever he does after this.[1]

However much people were able to benefit from the blessings of the Holy Prophet ﷺ, they became equivalent embodiments of sacrifice and spending in the path of Allah. This feature from the lives of the Companion was the effect of and the testimony to the Holy Prophet's teachings and perfect practical model. This was the practice and example of the Companions which is why they became exemplars for humanity. This sacrifice of theirs not only made them successful in gaining the pleasure of Allah, but those who follow them will also be successful in accomplishing their vision.

---

[1] Narrated by al-Tirmidhī in *al-Jāmiʿ al-Ṣaḥīḥ*, 5:625 §3700.

Q.101. WHO IS A GENEROUS PERSON (*SAKHĪ*)?

A: A generous person (*sakhī*) is a person who spends abundantly in the path of Allah. Qays b. Salaᶜ al-Anṣārī narrates:

أَنَّ إِخْوَتَهُ شَكَوْهُ إِلَى رَسُولِ اللهِ ﷺ، فَقالُوا: إِنَّهُ يُبَذِّرُ مَالَهُ وَيَنْبَسِطُ فِيهِ، فَقَالَ لَهُ رَسُولُ اللهِ ﷺ: يَا قَيْسُ، مَا شَأْنُ إِخْوَتِكَ يَشْكُونَكَ؟ يَزْعُمُونَ أَنَّكَ تُبَذِّرُ مَالَكَ وَتَنْبَسِطُ فِيه. قُلْتُ: يَا رَسُولَ اللهِ، إِنِّي آخُذُ نَصِيبِي مِنَ التَّمْرَةِ، فَأُنْفِقُهُ فِي سَبِيلِ اللهِ وَعَلَى مَنْ صَحِبَنِي قَالَ: فَضَرَبَ رَسُولُ اللهِ ﷺ صَدْرَهُ، فَقَالَ: أَنْفِق، يُنْفِقِ اللهُ عَلَيْكَ. ثَلَاثَ مَرَّاتٍ. فَلَمَّا كَانَ بَعْدَ ذَلِكَ خَرَجْتُ فِي سَبِيلِ اللهِ وَمَعِيَ رَاحِلَةٌ، وَقَالَ: أَنَا أَكْثَرُ أَهْلِ بَيْتِي الْيَوْمَ وَأَيْسَرُهُ.

His brothers complained about him to the Holy Prophet ﷺ. They asked, 'He wastes his wealth and he is happy with that.' The Holy Prophet ﷺ then asked him, 'Qays! What is the matter? Your brothers are complaining about you. They think you waste your money and you are happy with that.' He replied, 'O Messenger of Allah! I take my share from the produce and spend it in the path of Allah and on my friends.' The Holy Prophet ﷺ tapped his chest and said, 'You carry on spending, Allah will continue to spend on you.' The Holy Prophet ﷺ repeated this three times. After this when I set out in the path of Allah, my condition was that I had one ride, and

> today I am the wealthiest and the most well-off amongst all of my extended family.[1]

Q.102. WHAT IS THE REWARD OF A GENEROUS PERSON (*SAKHĪ*)?

A: The reward for a generous person is unlimited provision and Paradise. It is narrated from Abū Hurayra that the Holy Prophet ﷺ said:

> *Al-Sakhā* is a tree in Paradise. The person who is generous (*sakhī*), he will grasp one of its branches by which he will enter into Paradise.[2]

Abū Hurayra narrates that the Holy Prophet ﷺ said:

> قَالَ اللهُ: أَنْفِقْ أُنْفِقْ عَلَيْكَ. وَقَالَ: يَدُ اللهِ مَلأَى لاَ تَغِيضُهَا نَفَقَةٌ، سَحَّاءُ اللَّيْلَ وَالنَّهَارَ. وَقَالَ: أَرَأَيْتُمْ مَا أَنْفَقَ مُنْذُ خَلَقَ السَّمَاءَ وَالأَرْضَ فَإِنَّهُ لَمْ يَغِضْ مَا فِي يَدِهِ.

> Allah said, "Spend and I shall spend on you." He also said, "Allah's Hand is full, and (its fullness) is not affected by the continuous spending night and day." He also said, "Do you see what He has spent since He created the Heavens and the Earth? Nevertheless, what is in His Hand is not decreased."[3]

---

[1] Narrated by al-Ṭabarānī in *al-Muʿjam al-awsaṭ*, 8:246-247 §8536.
[2] Narrated by al-Bayhaqī in *Shuʿab al-īmān*, 7:435 §10,877.
[3] Narrated by al-Bukhārī in *al-Ṣaḥīḥ*, 4:1724 §4407; Muslim in *al-Ṣaḥīḥ*, 2:690 §993; Aḥmad b. Ḥanbal in *al-Musnad*, 2:313 §8125 and 2:500 §10,507; and Ibn Mājah in *al-Sunan*, 1:71 §197.

Q.103. WHAT IS THE BENEFIT OF CONTENTMENT?

A: The benefit of contentment (*qanāʿa*) are mentioned in the hadith narrated by ʿAbd Allāh b. ʿAmr b. al-Āṣ. He states that the Holy Prophet ﷺ said:

قَدْ أَفْلَحَ مَنْ هُدِيَ إِلَى الْإِسْلَامِ، وَرُزِقَ الْكَفَافَ وَقَنَعَ بِهِ.

> Successful is he who is guided to Islam and is content with the little provision he has.[1]

It is narrated that once Prophet Musa ﷺ asked, 'O Allah! Who is the wealthiest from amongst your servants?', and Allah ﷻ answered:

أَقْنَعُهُمْ بِمَا أَعْطَيْتُهُ.

> The one who is most content with what I have provided him.[2]

Dhū al-Nūn al-Miṣrī stated:

> Whoever is content, he receives comfort from the people and remains in control of his hands.[3]

It should be noted that contentment (*qanāʿa*) does not at all mean that the struggle to improve and progress should be relinquished. In fact the propagation of Islam, the collective wellbeing of Muslims, and the progress to the fore internationally reflects the core of Islam. However, total concentration and involvement in personal luxury and comfort is not advised and is against the teachings of Islam. The way in which the Holy Prophet ﷺ and the Rightly Guided Caliphs lived their lives, it is clear that their night and day was full of simplicity, hunger and

---

[1] Narrated by Ibn Mājah in *al-Sunan*, 4:483 §4138.
[2] Narrated by Ibn Sunnī in *Kitāb al-qanāʿa*.
[3] Al-Qushayrī in *al-Risāla*, p. 161.

poverty yet they always remained active in struggling to spread the religion of Islam.

Q.104. What is meant by a miser?

A: Someone who hoards wealth and does not spend it in the path of Allah is known as a miser (*bakhīl*). It is narrated by Abū Saʿīd al-Khudrī that the Holy Prophet ﷺ said:

خَصْلَتَانِ لَا تَجْتَمِعَانِ فِي مُؤْمِنٍ: الْـبُخْلُ، وَسُوءُ الْـخُلُقِ.

> Two features do not gather in a believer: miserliness and bad character.[1]

Asmāʾ narrates that the Holy Prophet ﷺ said to her:

أَنْفِقِي وَلَا تُحْصِي فَيُحْصِيَ اللهُ عَلَيْكِ وَلَا تُوعِي فَيُوعِيَ اللهُ عَلَيْكِ.

> Spend and do not give reluctantly, otherwise Allah will provide you reluctantly; and do not withhold lest Allah withholds from you.[2]

Ḥasan b. Abū al-Ḥasan narrates that the Holy Prophet ﷺ once related a *ḥadīth qudsī* in which Allah ﷻ said:

يَا ابْنَ آدَمَ، أَوْدِعْ مِنْ كَنْزِكَ عِنْدِي. وَلَا حَرَقَ وَلَا غَرَقَ وَلَا سَرَقَ أُوتِيكَهُ أَحْوَجَ مَا تَكُونُ إِلَيْهِ.

> O son of Ādam! Deposit a portion of your treasure with me. It will not burn, nor sink, nor

---

[1] Narrated by al-Tirmidhī in *al-Jāmiʿ al-Ṣaḥīḥ*, 4:343 §1962; al-Yaʿlā in *al-Musnad*, 2:490 §328; al-Ṭayālasī in *al-Musnad*, 1:293 §2208; and al-Bayhaqī in *Shuʿab al-īmān*, 7:423 §10,830.

[2] Narrated by al-Bukhārī in *al-Ṣaḥīḥ*, 2:915 §2451; Muslim in *al-Ṣaḥīḥ*, 2:713 §1029; and Aḥmad b. Ḥanbal in *al-Musnad*, 6:345 §26,967.

will it get stolen. When you are in dire need of it, I will return it to you.[1]

Q.105. WHAT WARNING HAS BEEN GIVEN TO THE MISER?

A: The miser (*bakhīl*) has been warned in the Qurʾān and hadith about the destruction of his wealth. Allah ﷻ states:

﴿وَأَمَّا مَنۢ بَخِلَ وَٱسۡتَغۡنَىٰ ۝٨ وَكَذَّبَ بِٱلۡحُسۡنَىٰ ۝٩ فَسَنُيَسِّرُهُۥ لِلۡعُسۡرَىٰ ۝١٠ وَمَا يُغۡنِي عَنۡهُ مَالُهُۥٓ إِذَا تَرَدَّىٰٓ﴾

But he who is miser and disregards (spending in the cause of Allah), and (in this way) denies the good (the Din [Religion]) of truth and afterlife), soon shall We facilitate his landing into hardship (advancing towards torment, so that punishment becomes his rightful due), and his wealth will not help him any way when he falls into (the pit of) destruction.[2]

1. Abū Hurayra narrates that the Holy Prophet ﷺ said:

مَا مِنْ يَوْمٍ يُصْبِحُ الْعِبَادُ فِيهِ إِلَّا مَلَكَانِ يَنْزِلَانِ فَيَقُولُ أَحَدُهُمَا: اللَّهُمَّ أَعْطِ مُنْفِقًا خَلَفًا؛ وَيَقُولُ الآخَرُ اللَّهُمَّ أَعْطِ مُمْسِكًا تَلَفًا.

Every day two angels come down from Heaven and one of them says, 'O Allah! Compensate every person who spends in Your cause,' and the other angel says, 'O Allah! Destroy every miser.'[3]

---

[1] Narrated by al-Bayhaqī in *Shuʿab al-īmān*, 3:221 §2342; and al-Hindī in *Kanz al-ʿummāl*, 6:151 §16,021.
[2] Qurʾān 92:8-11.
[3] Narrated by al-Bukhārī in *al-Ṣaḥīḥ*, 2:522 §1374; and Muslim in *al-Ṣaḥīḥ*, 2:700 §1010.

2. In another narration, Abū Hurayra narrates that the Holy Prophet ﷺ said:

مَثَلُ الْبَخِيلِ وَالْـمُنْفِقِ كَمَثَلِ رَجُلَيْنِ، عَلَيْهِمَا جُبَّتَانِ مِنْ حَدِيدٍ، مِنْ ثُدِيِّهِمَا إِلَى تَرَاقِيهِمَا. فَأَمَّا الْـمُنْفِقُ فَلاَ يُنْفِقُ إِلاَّ سَبَغَتْ (أَوْ وَفَرَتْ) عَلَى جِلْدِهِ حَتَّى تُخْفِيَ بَنَانَهُ وَتَعْفُوَ أَثَرَهُ. وَأَمَّا الْبَخِيلُ فَلاَ يُرِيدُ أَنْ يُنْفِقَ شَيْئًا إِلاَّ لَزِقَتْ كُلُّ حَلْقَةٍ مَكَانَهَا، فَهُوَ يُوَسِّعُهَا وَلاَ تَتَّسِعُ.

The example of an almsgiver and a miser is like the example of two persons who have two iron cloaks on them from their breasts to their collar bones. When the almsgiver wants to give in charity, the cloak becomes capacious till it covers his whole body to such an extent that it hides his fingertips and covers his footprints (obliterates his tracks); and when the miser wants to spend, it (the iron cloak) sticks and every ring gets stuck to its place and he tries to widen it, but it did not become wide.[1]

3. Abū Bakr al-Ṣiddīq ﷺ narrates that the Holy Prophet ﷺ said:

لَا يَدْخُلُ الْـجَنَّةَ خِبٌّ، وَلَا مَنَّانٌ، وَلَا بَـخِيلٌ.

A deceitful person, a person who boasts his favours on others and a miser will not enter Paradise.[2]

---

[1] Narrated by al-Bukhārī in *al-Ṣaḥīḥ*, 2:523 §1375; and Muslim in *al-Ṣaḥīḥ*, 2:700 §1010.

[2] Narrated by Aḥmad b. Ḥanbal in *al-Musnad*, 1:7 §32; al-Tirmidhī in *al-Jāmiʿ al-Ṣaḥīḥ*, 4:343 §1963; and Abū Yaʿlā in *al-Musnad*, 1:95 §95.

4. ʿUmar b. al-Khaṭṭāb ﷺ narrates that the Holy Prophet ﷺ said:

اَلْـجَالِبُ مَرْزُوقٌ وَالْـمُحْتَكِرُ مَلْعُونٌ.

> One who imports good (for the sake of trade) is given provision; and the one who hoards (in order to raise prices) is cursed.[1]

Q.106. What is charity (*ṣadaqa*)?

A: Charity (*ṣadaqa*) is that property, wealth or asset that is given to the poor for the sake of Allah.[2]

Imam Rāghib al-Aṣfahānī writes:

> Charity (*ṣadaqa*) is that donation which is not obligatory but the donor intends the nearness of Allah by it.[3]

It is that extra donation that is given in surplus to the zakah, which is spent upon the poor in order to put an end to their economic inactivity, to reestablish their creativity so that they can play their positive role in the progress and development of society.

Q.107. What is the virtue of giving charity (*ṣadaqa*)?

A: Giving charity for the sake of Allah is not a personal accomplishment or triumph because the life and property one possesses is in reality a blessing from Allah. It is solely Allah's favour upon His servants that he accepts the charity they donate and returns it to them by multiplying it many folds. He also provides to all endlessly. The Qurʾān and hadith mention the virtues of giving charity,

---

[1] Narrated by Ibn Mājah in *al-Sunan*, 3:11-12 §2153.
[2] Ibn Manẓūr, *Lisān al-ʿArab*, 10:196.
[3] Rāghib al-Aṣfahānī, *al-Mufradāt*, p. 480.

in fact it has been declared as a means of attaining the pleasure of Allah and His Messenger. This clear and totally unambiguous truth is mentioned in the Qur'ān through a glorious example:

﴿وَمَثَلُ ٱلَّذِينَ يُنفِقُونَ أَمْوَٰلَهُمُ ٱبْتِغَآءَ مَرْضَاتِ ٱللَّهِ وَتَثْبِيتًا مِّنْ أَنفُسِهِمْ كَمَثَلِ جَنَّةٍۭ بِرَبْوَةٍ أَصَابَهَا وَابِلٌ فَـَٔاتَتْ أُكُلَهَا ضِعْفَيْنِ فَإِن لَّمْ يُصِبْهَا وَابِلٌ فَطَلٌّ ۗ وَٱللَّهُ بِمَا تَعْمَلُونَ بَصِيرٌ﴾

And those who spend their wealth to seek Allah's pleasure and stabilize themselves (in faith and obedience) are like a garden located on a higher ground level. When a heavy rain falls on it, it doubles its yield. And if it does not receive a heavy rain, then even dew (or drizzle) is sufficient. And Allah monitors your actions minutely.[1]

This concept is also explained in another place in the Qur'ān:

﴿وَمِنَ ٱلْأَعْرَابِ مَن يُؤْمِنُ بِٱللَّهِ وَٱلْيَوْمِ ٱلْءَاخِرِ وَيَتَّخِذُ مَا يُنفِقُ قُرُبَٰتٍ عِندَ ٱللَّهِ وَصَلَوَٰتِ ٱلرَّسُولِ ۚ أَلَآ إِنَّهَا قُرْبَةٌ لَّهُمْ ۚ سَيُدْخِلُهُمُ ٱللَّهُ فِى رَحْمَتِهِۦٓ ۗ إِنَّ ٱللَّهَ غَفُورٌ رَّحِيمٌ ﴿٩٩﴾ وَٱلسَّٰبِقُونَ ٱلْأَوَّلُونَ مِنَ ٱلْمُهَٰجِرِينَ وَٱلْأَنصَارِ وَٱلَّذِينَ ٱتَّبَعُوهُم بِإِحْسَٰنٍ رَّضِىَ ٱللَّهُ عَنْهُمْ وَرَضُوا۟ عَنْهُ وَأَعَدَّ لَهُمْ جَنَّٰتٍ تَجْرِى تَحْتَهَا ٱلْأَنْهَٰرُ خَٰلِدِينَ فِيهَآ أَبَدًا ۚ ذَٰلِكَ ٱلْفَوْزُ ٱلْعَظِيمُ﴾

And (yet) amongst these nomads there is (also) one who believes in Allah and the Last Day and considers whatever he spends (in the way of

---

[1] Qur'ān 2:265.

Allah) as a means of nearness to Allah and receiving (the merciful) supplications of the Messenger. Listen! Assuredly, it is a source of nearness to Allah. Allah will soon admit them to His mercy. Surely, Allah is Most Forgiving, Ever-Merciful. And the Emigrants and their Supporters (Ansar), the vanguard of the believers, and those who follow them in the grade of spiritual excellence—Allah is well-pleased with them (all) and they (all) are well-pleased with Him. And He has prepared for them Gardens with rivers flowing under them. They will live in them forever. This is indeed a colossal achievement.[1]

The first verse has declared the obligatory charity (*ṣadaqa wājiba*) as the means of gaining the nearness and pleasure of Allah and His Messenger. The second verse aligns this practice with *iḥsān* declaring it to be the true basis of Allah's pleasure. Similarly the virtues of charity have been mentioned many a times in the hadiths. A few of these hadiths are related below.

1. Abū Hurayra narrates that the Holy Prophet ﷺ said:

مَا نَقَصَتْ صَدَقَةٌ مِنْ مَالٍ، وَمَا زَادَ اللهُ عَبْدًا بِعَفْوٍ إِلَّا عِزًّا، وَمَا تَوَاضَعَ أَحَدٌ لِلهِ إِلَّا رَفَعَهُ اللهُ.

Charity does not decrease one's wealth. When a servant forgives, his honour is increased; and no one humbles himself for the sake of Allah, except

[1] Qur'ān 9:99-100.

that Allah raises him (in the estimation of people).[1]

2. Anas b. Mālik narrates that the Holy Prophet ﷺ said:

إِنَّ الصَّدَقَةَ لَتُطْفِئُ غَضَبَ الرَّبِّ، وَتَدْفَعُ عَنْ مِيتَةِ السُّوءِ.

Charity cools the wrath of Allah and prevents a bad death.[2]

In connection to this, Imam al-Ṭabarānī relates:

عَنْ كَثِيرِ بْنِ عَبْدِ اللهِ الْمُزَنِيِّ عَنْ أَبِيهِ عَنْ جَدِّهِ قَالَ: قَالَ رَسُولُ اللهِ ﷺ: إِنَّ صَدَقَةَ الْمُسْلِمِ تَزِيدُ فِي الْعُمْرِ وَتَمْنَعُ مِيتَةَ السُّوءِ، وَيُذْهِبُ اللهُ بِهَا الْكِبْرَ وَالْفَخْرَ.

Kathīr b. ʿAbd Allāh al-Muzanī narrates from his father who narrates from his grandfather that the Holy Prophet ﷺ said: "A Muslim's charity increases his age, prevents a bad death, and through it Allah eliminates pride and arrogance."[3]

3. Rāfiʿ b. Khadīj narrates that the Messenger of Allah ﷺ said:

الصَّدَقَةُ تَسُدُّ سَبْعِينَ بَابًا مِنَ السُّوءِ.

---

[1] Narrated by Muslim in *al-Ṣaḥīḥ*, 4:2001 §2588; al-Dārimī in *al-Sunan*, 1:486 §1676; Ibn Khuzayma in *al-Ṣaḥīḥ*, 4:97 §2438; and Abū Yaʿlā in *al-Musnad*, 11:344 §6458.

[2] Narrated by al-Tirmidhī in *al-Jāmiʿ al-Ṣaḥīḥ*, 3:52 §664; Ibn Ḥibbān in *al-Ṣaḥīḥ*, 8:103 §3309; al-Bayhaqī in *Shuʿab al-īmān*, 3:213 §3351; and al-Maqdasī in *al-Aḥādīth al-mukhtāra*, 5:218 §1897.

[3] Narrated by al-Ṭabarānī in *al-Muʿjam al-kabīr*, 17:22 §31.

Charity blocks seventy doors of misfortune.[1]

4. ʿUqba narrates that the Holy Prophet ﷺ said:

إِنَّ الصَّدَقَةَ لَتُطْفِئُ عَنْ أَهْلِهَا حَرَّ الْقُبُورِ، وَإِنَّمَا يَسْتَظِلُّ الْمُؤْمِنُ يَوْمَ الْقِيَامَةِ فِي ظِلِّ صَدَقَتِهِ.

Charity extinguishes the heat of the grave and the believer is only shaded by his charity on the Day of Judgement.[2]

5. Maymūna bint Saʿd narrates that she asked the Prophet, 'O Messenger of Allah, inform us about charity', so the Holy Prophet ﷺ said:

إِنَّهَا حِجَابٌ مِنَ النَّارِ لِمَنِ احْتَسَبَهَا يَبْتَغِي بِهَا وَجْهَ اللهِ.

Indeed it is a veil from the fire for whoever spends seeking the pleasure of Allah.[3]

It is clear from these hadiths that there is immense virtue in donating charity. The nearness and pleasure of Allah can be attained by it and it is a means of extending one's life. Not only does it prevent difficulties and calamities, the dead also benefit from its blessings.

Q.108. Is it compulsory for every Muslim to give charity?

A: Yes, charity is compulsory on every Muslim, although there are different types of charity. It does not necessarily mean that wealth must be spent in order to gain the reward of charity as the concept of charity in Islam is very broad. The Holy Prophet ﷺ said:

---

[1] Ibid., 4:274 §4402.
[2] Ibid., 17:286 §787.
[3] Ibid., 25:35 §3449.

عَلَى كُلِّ مُسْلِمٍ صَدَقَةٌ.

Charity (*ṣadaqa*) is compulsory on every Muslim.

The Companions asked:

يَا نَبِيَّ اللهِ! فَمَنْ لَـمْ يَجِدْ؟

O Messenger of Allah! What if he cannot do so?

The Holy Prophet ﷺ replied:

يَعْمَلُ بِيَدِهِ فَيَنْفَعُ نَفْسَهُ وَيَتَصَدَّقُ.

He should labour and benefit himself and give in charity.

The Companions asked:

فَمَنْ لَـمْ يَجِدْ؟

What if he cannot do so?

The Holy Prophet ﷺ replied:

يُعِينُ ذَا الْـحَاجَةِ الْـمَلْهُوفَ.

He should aid a needy person who is in trouble.

The Companions asked:

فَإِنْ لَـمْ يَجِدْ؟

What if he cannot do so?

The Holy Prophet ﷺ replied:

فَلْيَعْمَلْ بِالْـمَعْرُوفِ وَلْيُمْسِكْ عَنِ الشَّرِّ فَإِنَّهَا لَهُ صَدَقَةٌ.

He should perform a good deed and abstain from evil, for indeed that is his charity.[1]

Therefore, it is clear that everyone should perform charity to the best of his or her ability, in whichever form possible.

Q.109. Should charity be given secretly or openly?

A: It is permissible to give charity discretely and openly. It is a means of forgiveness for sins. Allah ﷻ states:

﴿إِن تُبْدُوا۟ ٱلصَّدَقَـٰتِ فَنِعِمَّا هِىَ ۖ وَإِن تُخْفُوهَا وَتُؤْتُوهَا ٱلْفُقَرَآءَ فَهُوَ خَيْرٌ لَّكُمْ ۚ وَيُكَفِّرُ عَنكُم مِّن سَيِّـَٔاتِكُمْ ۗ وَٱللَّهُ بِمَا تَعْمَلُونَ خَبِيرٌ﴾

If you give charity in public, it is worthwhile (for it will persuade others), but if you hide and deliver it to the poor in secret, that is (far) better for you. And Allah will remove from you some of your sins (due to this charity). And Allah is Well Aware of all that you do.[2]

Ibn ʿAbbās interpreting this verse states that Allah made the act of giving voluntary charity in secret seventy (70) times more rewarding than giving it openly. Whereas giving obligatory charity (i.e., zakah and *ṣadaqa al-fiṭr*) secretly is fifteen (15) times more rewarding than giving it openly.[3]

Abū Dharr asked the Holy Prophet ﷺ which charity is the best to give. The Holy Prophet ﷺ said:

---

[1] Narrated by al-Bukhārī in *al-Ṣaḥīḥ*, 2:524 §1376.

[2] Qurʾān 2:271.

[3] Makkī b. Abī Ṭālib al-Muqriʾ, *Tafsīr al-hidāya ilā bulūgh al-nihāya*, 2:899; and al-Qurṭubī, *al-Jāmiʿ li-aḥkām al-Qurʾān*, 3:332.

سِرٌّ إِلَى فَقِيرٍ وَجُهْدٌ مِنْ مُقِلٍّ.

The secret giving to the poor and the strenuous effort of a destitute.[1]

Jābir b. ʿAbd Allāh narrates that the Holy Prophet ﷺ said during a sermon:

يَا أَيُّهَا النَّاسُ، تُوبُوا إِلَى اللهِ قَبْلَ أَنْ تَمُوتُوا، وَبَادِرُوا إِلَى اللهِ تَعَالَى بِالْأَعْمَالِ الصَّالِحَةِ، وَصِلُوا مَا بَيْنَكُمْ وَبَيْنَ رَبِّكُمْ بِكَثْرَةِ ذِكْرِكُمْ، وَكَثْرَةِ الصَّدَقَةِ فِي السِّرِّ وَالْعَلَانِيَةِ، تُرْزَقُوا، وَتُنْصَرُوا، وَتُجْبَرُوا.

O people, repent to Allah before you die; hasten to the performance of good deeds; create a link between you and your Lord with much remembrance and abundant charity secretly and in open, and you will be given provision and you will receive assistance.[2]

Anas b. Mālik narrates that the Holy Prophet ﷺ said:

لَمَّا خَلَقَ اللهُ الْأَرْضَ جَعَلَتْ تَمِيدُ فَخَلَقَ الْجِبَالَ فَعَادَ بِهَا عَلَيْهَا فَاسْتَقَرَّتْ فَعَجِبَتْ الْمَلَائِكَةُ مِنْ شِدَّةِ الْجِبَالِ. قَالُوا: يَا رَبِّ هَلْ مِنْ خَلْقِكَ شَيْءٌ أَشَدُّ مِنْ الْجِبَالِ. قَالَ: نَعَمْ الْحَدِيدُ. قَالُوا: يَا رَبِّ فَهَلْ مِنْ خَلْقِكَ شَيْءٌ أَشَدُّ مِنْ الْحَدِيدِ. قَالَ: نَعَمْ النَّارُ. فَقَالُوا: يَا رَبِّ فَهَلْ مِنْ خَلْقِكَ شَيْءٌ أَشَدُّ مِنْ النَّارِ. قَالَ: نَعَمْ الْمَاءُ. قَالُوا: يَا رَبِّ فَهَلْ مِنْ خَلْقِكَ شَيْءٌ أَشَدُّ مِنْ الْمَاءِ.

---

[1] Narrated by Aḥmad b. Ḥanbal in *al-Musnad*, 5:265 §22,644; and al-Ṭabarānī in *al-Muʿjam al-awsaṭ*, 8:217 §7871 and 8:226 §7891.
[2] Narrated by Ibn Mājah in *al-Sunan*, 1:343 §1081.

قَالَ: نَعَمْ الرِّيحُ. قَالُوا: يَا رَبِّ فَهَلْ مِنْ خَلْقِكَ شَيْءٌ أَشَدُّ مِنَ الرِّيحِ. قَالَ: نَعَمْ ابْنُ آدَمَ تَصَدَّقَ بِصَدَقَةٍ بِيَمِينِهِ يُخْفِيهَا مِنْ شِمَالِهِ.

> When Allah created the earth, it started shaking. So He created the mountains, and said to them: 'Upon it' so it began to settle. The angels were amazed at the strength of the mountains, so they said: 'O Lord! Is there among your creatures one who is more severe than the mountains?' He said: 'Yes. Iron.' They said: 'O Lord! Then is there anything among your creatures that is more severe than that iron?' He said: 'Yes. Fire.' They said: 'O Lord! Is there anything among your creatures that is more severe than fire?' He said: 'Yes. Water.' They said: 'O Lord! Is there anything among your creatures that is more severe than water?' He said: 'Yes. Wind.' They said: 'O Lord! Is there anything among your creatures more severe than wind?' He said: 'Yes, the son of Ādam. He gives charity with his right hands, while hiding it from his left.'[1]

It is better to perform the voluntary charity secretly, however it may be better to announce it due to a religious reason or in order to encourage and motivate others. Nevertheless it must be ensured that it is not done in order to show off; but if this is the case then the action will go to waste and will amount to sin instead. Therefore, if the charity is performed, whether it is

[1] Narrated by Aḥmad b. Ḥanbal in *al-Musnad*, 3:124 §12,275; al-Tirmidhī in *al-Jāmiʿ al-Ṣaḥīḥ*, 5:454 §3369; ʿAbd b. Ḥumayd in *al-Musnad*, 1:365 §1215; and al-Daylamī in *Musnad al-Firdaws*, 3:423 §5298.

obligatory or voluntary, if it is done with sincerity and not done to show off, then whether it is given openly or secretly, it is good—although it is better to reveal the zakah and to conceal the voluntary charity.

Q.110. What is the virtue of spending on one's family and relatives?

A: There are many virtues mentioned in the books of hadith regarding spending on one's family and relatives, if they are in need of it. In fact it is more rewarding to give one's *ṣadaqa* to one's family and relatives as opposed to those who are not related.

1. Abū Hurayra narrates that the Holy Prophet ﷺ said:

دِينَارٌ أَنْفَقْتَهُ فِي سَبِيلِ الله وَدِينَارٌ أَنْفَقْتَهُ فِي رَقَبَةٍ وَدِينَارٌ تَصَدَّقْتَ بِهِ عَلَى مِسْكِينٍ وَدِينَارٌ أَنْفَقْتَهُ عَلَى أَهْلِكَ أَعْظَمُهَا أَجْرًا الَّذِي أَنْفَقْتَهُ عَلَى أَهْلِكَ.

> Of the dinar you spend as a contribution in Allah's path, or to set free a slave, or as a charity given to a needy, or to support your family, the one yielding the greatest reward is that which you spent on your family.[1]

2. In another narration, Abū Hurayra narrates that he asked the Holy Prophet ﷺ, 'O Messenger of Allah, which charity is best?' The Holy Prophet ﷺ said:

جُهْدُ الْمُقِلِّ وَابْدَأْ بِمَنْ تَعُولُ.

---

[1] Narrated by Muslim in *al-Ṣaḥīḥ*, 2:692 §995; Aḥmad b. Ḥanbal in *al-Musnad*, 2:476 §10,177; al-Ṭabarānī in *al-Muʿjam al-awsaṭ*, 9:39 §9079; and al-Daylamī in *Musnad al-Firdaws*, 2:222 §3079.

It is the charity given by the strenuous earning of a poor person and to begin with those who are under your guardianship.[1]

3. Abū Hurayra also narrates:

أَمَرَ النَّبِيُّ ﷺ بِالصَّدَقَةِ. فَقَالَ رَجُلٌ: يَا رَسُولَ اللهِ عِنْدِي دِينَارٌ. فَقَالَ: تَصَدَّقْ بِهِ عَلَى نَفْسِكَ. قَالَ عِنْدِي آخَرُ. قَالَ: تَصَدَّقْ بِهِ عَلَى وَلَدِكَ. قَالَ عِنْدِي آخَرُ. قَالَ: تَصَدَّقْ بِهِ عَلَى زَوْجَتِكَ. أَوْ قَالَ: زَوْجِكَ. قَالَ عِنْدِي آخَرُ. قَالَ: تَصَدَّقْ بِهِ عَلَى خَادِمِكَ. قَالَ عِنْدِي آخَرُ . قَالَ: أَنْتَ أَبْصَرُ.

The Holy Prophet ﷺ commanded to give charity. A man said, "O Messenger of Allah, I have a dinar." He said: "Spend it on yourself." He again said: "I have another." He said: "Spend it on your children." He again said: "I have another." He said: "Spend it on your wife." He again said: "I have another." He said: "Spend it on your servant." He finally said: "I have another." He replied: "You know best (what to do with it)."[2]

4. Salmān b. ʿĀmir narrates that the Holy Prophet ﷺ said:

---

[1] Narrated by Aḥmad b. Ḥanbal in *al-Musnad*, 2:358 §8687; Abū Dāwūd in *al-Sunan*, 2:129 §1677; Ibn Ḥibbān in *al-Ṣaḥīḥ*, 8:134 §3346; Ibn Khuzayma in *al-Ṣaḥīḥ*, 4:102 §2451; and al-Ḥākim in *al-Mustadrak*, 1:574 §1509.

[2] Narrated by Abū Dāwūd in *al-Sunan*, 2:132 §1691; al-Nasāʾī in *al-Sunan*, 5:62 §2535; al-Ḥākim in *al-Mustadrak*, 1:585 §1514; Ibn Ḥibbān in *al-Ṣaḥīḥ*, 8:126 §3337; al-Bukhārī in *al-Adab al-mufrad*, 1:78 §197; and al-Ṭabarānī in *al-Muʿjam al-awsaṭ*, 8:237 §8508.

الصَّدَقَةُ عَلَى الْـمِسْكِينِ صَدَقَةٌ وَهِيَ عَلَى ذِي الرَّحِمِ ثِنْتَانِ: صَدَقَةٌ وَصِلَةٌ.

> Giving charity to a destitute is a *ṣadaqa*, yet giving charity to one's family relations amounts to twice the reward: (the reward of) *ṣadaqa* and maintaining family ties.[1]

In our times, there is a prevalent problem where people spend abundantly on non-relatives by giving them their charity but overlook their own relatives who may be poor and deserving. This kind of reasoning is not proper and it is mainly based on seeing others negatively and due to arrogance. For example, a poor relative displeases his wealthy relative by differing with his views or merely speaking about him, resulting in the wealthy relative building up resentment against the other thus neglecting to help his poor relative. In doing so he deprives himself of double reward. From this it is safe to say that people prioritise who they want to give charity to on the basis of their personal preferences and not according to the dictates of the Shariah.

Sometimes the aim is to make the poor person indebted to one's person as opposed to acting upon the rulings of Allah ﷻ. In the end this results in the neglect of one's poor relatives. Not just charity, all our practices and deeds should be performed solely for the sake of Allah and to attain His pleasure. This should be the ultimate purpose of one's actions—not one's personal likings.

---

[1] Narrated by al-Tirmidhī in *al-Jāmiʿ al-Ṣaḥīḥ*, 5:92 §2582; Ibn Mājah in *al-Sunan*, 1:591 §1844; al-Ḥākim in *al-Mustadrak*, 1:564 §1476; and Ibn Khuzayma in *al-Ṣaḥīḥ*, 8:132 §3344.

Q.111. WHAT IS THE RULING ON CHARITY BEING GIVEN FOR THE SAKE OF SHOWING OFF TO OTHERS?

A: Charity which is donated for the sake of gaining fame and respect will not be accepted by Allah, but it will rather be a source of disgrace and anguish. Any pious or virtuous act carried out to show off to others or for personal veneration will never be accepted rather there is a severe warning on this. The Qur'ān states:

﴿يَـٰٓأَيُّهَا ٱلَّذِينَ ءَامَنُوا۟ لَا تُبْطِلُوا۟ صَدَقَـٰتِكُم بِٱلْمَنِّ وَٱلْأَذَىٰ
كَٱلَّذِى يُنفِقُ مَالَهُۥ رِئَآءَ ٱلنَّاسِ وَلَا يُؤْمِنُ بِٱللَّهِ وَٱلْيَوْمِ ٱلْـَٔاخِرِ ۖ
فَمَثَلُهُۥ كَمَثَلِ صَفْوَانٍ عَلَيْهِ تُرَابٌ فَأَصَابَهُۥ وَابِلٌ فَتَرَكَهُۥ صَلْدًا ۖ لَّا
يَقْدِرُونَ عَلَىٰ شَىْءٍ مِّمَّا كَسَبُوا۟ ۗ وَٱللَّهُ لَا يَهْدِى ٱلْقَوْمَ ٱلْكَـٰفِرِينَ﴾

O believers! Do not ruin your charity donations (later) by taunts of doing favour and hurting feelings like the one who gives charity to show off his wealth to the people and believes in neither Allah nor the Last Day. His case is like a smooth rock covered with a thin coat of soil. Then heavy rain falls on it, washes it clean and leaves it (the same) bare and hard (rock). So these (pretentious people) shall get nothing out of their earning. And Allah does not guide the disbelievers.[1]

In a lengthy narration, Abū Hurayra relates that there were three types of people who will be thrown into the Hellfire. One such person will be a generous person who used to spend his wealth in order to show off. The Holy Prophet ﷺ said:

---

[1] Qur'ān 2:264.

إِنَّ أَوَّلَ النَّاسِ يُقْضَى يَوْمَ الْقِيَامَةِ عَلَيْهِ رَجُلٌ... وَسَّعَ اللهُ عَلَيْهِ وَأَعْطَاهُ مِنْ أَصْنَافِ الْـمَـالِ كُلِّهِ فَأُتِيَ بِهِ فَعَرَّفَهُ نِعَمَهُ فَعَرَفَهَا. قَالَ: فَمَـا عَمِلْتَ فِيهَا. قَالَ: مَا تَرَكْتُ مِنْ سَبِيلٍ تُحِبُّ أَنْ يُنْفَقَ فِيهَا إِلَّا أَنْفَقْتُ فِيهَا لَكَ. قَالَ: كَذَبْتَ وَلَكِنَّكَ فَعَلْتَ لِيُقَالَ هُوَ جَوَادٌ. فَقَدْ قِيلَ ثُمَّ أُمِرَ بِهِ فَسُحِبَ عَلَى وَجْهِهِ ثُمَّ أُلْقِيَ فِي النَّارِ.

The first of men (whose case) will be decided on the Day of Judgment will be a man... whom Allah ﷻ had made abundantly rich and had granted every kind of wealth. He will be brought and Allah will make him recount His blessings and he will recount them and (admit having enjoyed them in his lifetime). Allah ﷻ will (then) ask: "What have you done (to requite these blessings)?" He will say: "I spent money in every cause in which You wished that it should be spent." Allah ﷻ will say: "You are lying. You did so that it might be said about you: 'He is a generous fellow' and so it was said." Then Allah ﷻ will pass orders and he will be dragged with his face downward and thrown into Hell.[1]

Therefore, while spending in the path of Allah or performing any other virtuous act the intention should never be to be known as a pious and generous person. Such conduct not only renders the deed futile but is also liable to a penalty. Thus, when performing a virtuous act, the pleasure of Allah and His Messenger should always be

---

[1] Narrated by Muslim in *al-Ṣaḥīḥ*, 3:1514 §1905; Aḥmad b. Ḥanbal in *al-Musnad*, 2:321 §8260; al-Ḥākim in *al-Mustadrak*, 1:189 §364; Abū ʿAwāna in *al-Musnad*, 4:489 §7441; and al-Bayhaqī in *al-Sunan al-kubrā*, 9:168.

the motivation which will lead that act to be accepted as worthy of being rewarded.

Q.112. DOES ONE'S WEALTH DECREASE BY GIVING IT AWAY IN CHARITY?

A: No, wealth does not decrease by giving charity but it increases manifold and Allah ﷻ also raises the ranks of charitable people.

1. Abū Hurayra narrates that the Holy Prophet ﷺ said:

مَا نَقَصَتْ صَدَقَةٌ مِنْ مَالٍ، وَمَا زَادَ اللهُ عَبْدًا بِعَفْوٍ إِلَّا عِزًّا، وَمَا تَوَاضَعَ أَحَدٌ لِلهِ إِلَّا رَفَعَهُ اللهُ.

Charity does not decrease one's wealth. When a servant forgives, his honour is increased; and no one humbles himself for the sake of Allah, except that Allah raises him (in the estimation of people).[1]

2. In another narration, Abū Hurayra narrates that the Holy Prophet ﷺ said:

بَيْنَا رَجُلٌ بِفَلَاةٍ مِنَ الأَرْضِ فَسَمِعَ صَوْتًا فِي سَحَابَةٍ: اسْقِ حَدِيقَةَ فُلَانٍ. فَتَنَحَّى ذَلِكَ السَّحَابُ. فَأَفْرَغَ مَاءَهُ فِي حَرَّةٍ فَإِذَا شَرْجَةٌ مِنْ تِلْكَ الشِّرَاجِ قَدِ اسْتَوْعَبَتْ ذَلِكَ الْمَاءَ كُلَّهُ فَتَتَبَّعَ الْمَاءَ فَإِذَا رَجُلٌ قَائِمٌ فِي حَدِيقَتِهِ يُحَوِّلُ الْمَاءَ بِمِسْحَاتِهِ. فَقَالَ لَهُ: يَا عَبْدَ اللهِ مَا اسْمُكَ قَالَ فُلَانٌ. لِلِاسْمِ الَّذِي سَمِعَ فِي السَّحَابَةِ. فَقَالَ لَهُ: يَا عَبْدَ اللهِ لِمَ تَسْأَلُنِي عَنِ اسْمِي. فَقَالَ: إِنِّي سَمِعْتُ صَوْتًا فِي

[1] Narrated by Muslim in *al-Ṣaḥīḥ*, 4:2001 §2588; al-Dārimī in *al-Sunan*, 1:486 §1676; Ibn Khuzayma in *al-Ṣaḥīḥ*, 4:97 §2438; and Abū Yaʿlā in *al-Musnad*, 11:344 §6458.

السَّحَابِ الَّذِي هَذَا مَاؤُهُ يَقُولُ اسْقِ حَدِيقَةَ فُلَانٍ لِاسْمِكَ فَمَا تَصْنَعُ فِيهَا. قَالَ: أَمَّا إِذَا قُلْتَ هَذَا فَإِنِّي أَنْظُرُ إِلَى مَا يَخْرُجُ مِنْهَا فَأَتَصَدَّقُ بِثُلُثِهِ وَآكُلُ أَنَا وَعِيَالِي ثُلُثًا وَأَرُدُّ فِيهَا ثُلُثَهُ.

A person whilst he was in the wilderness heard a voice from the cloud telling him to irrigate the garden of so and so. After that the clouds slinked aside and poured water on a stony ground. It filled a channel amongst the channels of that land and that person followed that water and he found a person standing in the garden busy in changing the course of water with the help of a hatchet. He said to him, "Servant of Allah, what is your name?" He said: "So and so." And it was that very name which he had heard from the clouds. He said to him: "Servant of Allah, why do you ask me my name?" He said: "I heard a voice from the clouds of which is the downpour, saying: 'Water the garden of so and so, like your name.' What do you do (for the favour) shown to you by Allah in this matter?" He said: "Now as you state so. I look what yield I get from it, and I give one-third as charity out of it and I and my children eat one-third of it and one-third I return to it as investment."[1]

Giving charity in the path of Allah in order to gain His pleasure results in receiving reward, one's rank is elevated, wealth is immensely blessed and assistance is provided through unseen means.

---

[1] Narrated by Muslim in *al-Ṣaḥīḥ*, 4:2288 §2984; Aḥmad b. Ḥanbal in *al-Musnad*, 2:296 §7928; and Ibn Ḥibbān in *al-Ṣaḥīḥ*, 8:142 §3355.

Q.113. Is every good deed a charity?

A: Yes, every virtuous act is an act of charity. It is narrated by Jābir b. ʿAbd Allāh that the Holy Prophet ﷺ said:

كُلُّ مَعْرُوفٍ صَدَقَةٌ.

Every good deed is a charity.[1]

2. Abū Dharr narrates that some of the Companions asked the Holy Prophet ﷺ:

يَا رَسُولَ اللهِ ذَهَبَ أَهْلُ الدُّثُورِ بِالأُجُورِ يُصَلُّونَ كَمَا نُصَلِّي وَيَصُومُونَ كَمَا نَصُومُ وَيَتَصَدَّقُونَ بِفُضُولِ أَمْوَالِهِمْ.

O Messenger of Allah! The wealthy have taken all the reward: they pray as we pray, they fast as we fast, and they give charity from the surplus of their wealth.

Hearing this the Holy Prophet ﷺ said:

أَوَلَيْسَ قَدْ جَعَلَ اللهُ لَكُمْ مَا تَصَّدَّقُونَ إِنَّ بِكُلِّ تَسْبِيحَةٍ صَدَقَةً وَكُلِّ تَكْبِيرَةٍ صَدَقَةٌ وَكُلِّ تَحْمِيدَةٍ صَدَقَةٌ وَكُلِّ تَهْلِيلَةٍ صَدَقَةٌ وَأَمْرٌ بِالْمَعْرُوفِ صَدَقَةٌ وَنَهْيٌ عَنْ مُنْكَرٍ صَدَقَةٌ وَفِي بُضْعِ أَحَدِكُمْ صَدَقَةٌ.

Has Allah ﷻ not given you an opportunity to perform charity? Every *tasbīḥ* is a charity; every *takbīr* is a charity; every *taḥmīd* is a charity; every *tahlīl* is a charity; commanding the good is

---

[1] Narrated by al-Bukhārī in *al-Ṣaḥīḥ*, 5:2241 §5675; and Muslim in *al-Ṣaḥīḥ*, 2:697 §1005.

a charity; forbidding the wrong is charity; and (even) marital relations is a charity.

The Companions further asked, 'O Messenger of Allah! If one satisfies his sexual desires (with his wife) is there reward in that too?', and the Holy Prophet ﷺ replied:

أَرَأَيْتُمْ لَوْ وَضَعَهَا فِي حَرَامٍ أَكَانَ عَلَيْهِ فِيهَا وِزْرٌ فَكَذَلِكَ إِذَا وَضَعَهَا فِي الْحَلَالِ كَانَ لَهُ أَجْرٌ.

Tell me if he had fulfilled his desire through unlawful means, would he not be sinful? Likewise if he satisfies it through lawful means there is reward in that.[1]

3. Abū Hurayra narrates that the Holy Prophet ﷺ:

كُلُّ سُلَامَى مِنَ النَّاسِ عَلَيْهِ صَدَقَةٌ كُلَّ يَوْمٍ تَطْلُعُ فِيهِ الشَّمْسُ، يَعْدِلُ بَيْنَ الاِثْنَيْنِ صَدَقَةٌ، وَيُعِينُ الرَّجُلَ عَلَى دَابَّتِهِ، فَيَحْمِلُ عَلَيْهَا، أَوْ يَرْفَعُ عَلَيْهَا مَتَاعَهُ صَدَقَةٌ، وَالْكَلِمَةُ الطَّيِّبَةُ صَدَقَةٌ، وَكُلُّ خَطْوَةٍ يَخْطُوهَا إِلَى الصَّلَاةِ صَدَقَةٌ، وَيُمِيطُ الأَذَى عَنِ الطَّرِيقِ صَدَقَةٌ.

There is a compulsory charity to be given for every joint of the human body every day the sun rises: to judge justly between two persons is a charity; to help a man on his riding animal by helping him to ride it or by lifting his luggage on to it, is also a charity; saying a good word is also a charity; every step taken towards the prayer is

[1] Narrated by Muslim in *al-Ṣaḥīḥ*, 2:697 §1006.

also a charity; and to remove a harmful object from the pathway is also a charity.[1]

The hadiths discussed above give the broad concept of charity that in Islam every good deed falls into the category of charity one way or another.

Q.114. WHAT IS CONTINUOUS CHARITY?

A: Continuous charity (*al-ṣadaqa al-jāriya*) refers to such a good deed, the benefit of which is continuous and the reward for it will be given to the person who performs that act throughout his life and after it. If people continue to benefit from it, he will continue to receive reward for it, without the reward of those people benefitting from it being reduced.

1. Abū Hurayra narrates that the Holy Prophet ﷺ:

إِنَّ مِمَّا يَلْحَقُ الْمُؤْمِنَ مِنْ عَمَلِهِ وَحَسَنَاتِهِ بَعْدَ مَوْتِهِ عِلْمًا عَلَّمَهُ وَنَشَرَهُ وَوَلَدًا صَالِحًا تَرَكَهُ وَمُصْحَفًا وَرَّثَهُ أَوْ مَسْجِدًا بَنَاهُ أَوْ بَيْتًا لِابْنِ السَّبِيلِ بَنَاهُ أَوْ نَهْرًا أَجْرَاهُ أَوْ صَدَقَةً أَخْرَجَهَا مِنْ مَالِهِ فِي صِحَّتِهِ وَحَيَاتِهِ يَلْحَقُهُ مِنْ بَعْدِ مَوْتِهِ.

The rewards of the good deeds that will reach a believer after his death are: knowledge which he taught and spread; a righteous son whom he leaves behind; a copy of the Qurʾān that he leaves as a legacy; a mosque that he built; a house that he built for wayfarers; a canal that he dug; or charity that he gave during his lifetime

[1] Narrated by al-Bukhārī in *al-Ṣaḥīḥ*, 3:1090 §2827.

when he was in good health. These deeds will reach him after his death.[1]

It should be noted that in the performance of any virtuous deed, if during someone's life or after death, if others also take part in it, then there will be no reduction in their reward. For example, if someone builds a mosque, he will continue to receive the reward for building it and the people praying there will also receive their reward. In the same way if someone spends in the path of Allah in order to build an inn that provides free lodging for travellers then the person who built it would continue to receive its reward. If someone has installed a water cooler for the general public then as long as people continue to drink water from it, he will continue to receive its reward. If someone built an ablution area for people to perform *wuḍū*ʾ, then he continues to receive reward so long as people continue to use it to perform *wuḍū*ʾ. If he dies, his reward will continue even after his death.

2. Abū Hurayra narrates that the Holy Prophet ﷺ:

إِذَا مَاتَ الإِنْسَانُ انْقَطَعَ عَنْهُ عَمَلُهُ إِلَّا مِنْ ثَلاَثَةٍ: إِلَّا مِنْ صَدَقَةٍ جَارِيَةٍ أَوْ عِلْمٍ يُنْتَفَعُ بِهِ أَوْ وَلَدٍ صَالِحٍ يَدْعُو لَهُ.

When a person dies his actions are terminated except for three: continuous charity (*al-ṣadaqa al-jāriya*), beneficial knowledge, and a righteous child who prays for him.[2]

---

[1] Narrated by Ibn Mājah in *al-Sunan*, 1:88 §242; Ibn Khuzayma in *al-Ṣaḥīḥ*, 4:121 §2490; and al-Bayhaqī in *Shuʿab al-īmān*, 3:248 §3448.

[2] Narrated by Muslim in *al-Ṣaḥīḥ*, 3:1255 §1631; Aḥmad b. Ḥanbal in *al-Musnad*, 2:372 §8831; Abū Dāwūd in *al-Sunan*, 3:117 §2880; al-Nasāʾī in *al-Sunan*, 6:251 §3651; Abū Yaʿlā in *al-Musnad*, 11:343 §6457; and Abū ʿAwāna in *al-Musnad*, 3:495 §5824.

Q.115. What is *qarḍ ḥasana*?

A: *Qarḍ ḥasana* is a loan which is given to the poor and needy only for the pleasure of Allah, where no material benefit or interest is sought in return. The only intention is to seek reward in the life hereafter.

Q.116. What is the status of those who are lenient in reclaiming their loans?

A: In Islam, the act of being lenient in reclaiming one's loans by giving the debtor more time or writing off his debts has been earmarked for great reward. The Qur'ān states:

﴿وَإِن كَانَ ذُو عُسْرَةٍ فَنَظِرَةٌ إِلَىٰ مَيْسَرَةٍ ۚ وَأَن تَصَدَّقُوا خَيْرٌ لَّكُمْ إِن كُنتُمْ تَعْلَمُونَ﴾

And if a debtor is under financial stress, he should be given respite till he feels at ease to pay. And your forgoing (the loan) is better for you if you know (what significance it has in the sight of Allah to console the poor).[1]

It should be noted that whilst the act of lending *qarḍ ḥasana* is recommended, it is equally important that the debtor makes all efforts to return it. The reason being is that debt is such a thing that if a person passes away without repaying it, it must be taken out of the person's property and returned to the lender before the inheritance can be divided. Secondly, the debt is not written off automatically after death, nor is it forgiven unless the lender wishes to do so. Therefore, loans should only be taken when there is no other option and should be returned as soon as possible.

---

[1] Qur'ān 2:280.

Q.117. What virtues and merits are mentioned in the hadith for helping the poor and needy?

A: Islam emphasises greatly upon creating social relations. In order to create unity and mutual love and respect within society cooperation has been greatly highlighted. This is the reason why Islam holds great virtue for those who assist the poor and needy in society.

1. ʿAbd Allāh b. ʿUmar narrates that the Holy Prophet ﷺ said:

مَنْ كَانَ فِي حَاجَةِ أَخِيهِ كَانَ اللهُ فِي حَاجَتِهِ، وَمَنْ فَرَّجَ عَنْ مُسْلِمٍ كُرْبَةً فَرَّجَ اللهُ عَنْهُ كُرْبَةً مِنْ كُرُبَاتِ يَوْمِ الْقِيَامَةِ، وَمَنْ سَتَرَ مُسْلِمًا سَتَرَهُ اللهُ يَوْمَ الْقِيَامَةِ.

Whoever assists his brother, Allah ﷻ will assist him; and whoever alleviates a Muslim's difficulty, Allah ﷻ will alleviate his difficulty on the Day of Judgement; and whoever hides the fault of a Muslim, Allah ﷻ will hide his faults on the Day of Judgement.[1]

2. Abū Hurayra narrates that the Holy Prophet ﷺ said:

مَنْ نَفَّسَ عَنْ مُؤْمِنٍ كُرْبَةً مِنْ كُرَبِ الدُّنْيَا نَفَّسَ اللهُ عَنْهُ كُرْبَةً مِنْ كُرَبِ يَوْمِ الْقِيَامَةِ. وَمَنْ يَسَّرَ عَلَى مُعْسِرٍ يَسَّرَ اللهُ عَلَيْهِ فِي الدُّنْيَا وَالآخِرَةِ. وَمَنْ سَتَرَ مُسْلِمًا سَتَرَهُ اللهُ فِي الدُّنْيَا وَالآخِرَةِ وَاللهُ فِي عَوْنِ الْعَبْدِ مَا كَانَ الْعَبْدُ فِي عَوْنِ أَخِيهِ.

---

[1] Narrated by al-Bukhārī in *al-Ṣaḥīḥ*, 2:862 §2310; and Muslim in *al-Ṣaḥīḥ*, 4:1996 §2580.

Whoever alleviates a believer's difficulty in this world, Allah ﷻ will alleviate his difficulty on the Day of Judgement. Whoever finds relief for one who is hard-pressed, Allah ﷻ would make things easy for him in the life hereafter. Whoever hides the faults of a Muslim, Allah ﷻ will hide his faults in this life and the life hereafter. Allah ﷻ will continue to assist His servant so long as His servant assists his brother.[1]

3. Anas narrates that the Holy Prophet ﷺ said:

لَا يَزَالُ اللهُ فِي حَاجَةِ الْعَبْدِ مَا دَامَ فِي حَاجَةِ أَخِيهِ.

Allah ﷻ will continue to assist His servant so long as His servant assists his brother.[2]

4. ʿAbd Allāh b. ʿUmar narrates that the Holy Prophet ﷺ said:

إِنَّ لِلهِ خَلْقًا خَلَقَهُمْ لِحَوَائِجِ النَّاسِ يَفْزَعُ النَّاسُ إِلَيْهِمْ فِي حَوَائِجِهِمْ أُولَئِكَ الْآمِنُونَ مِنْ عَذَابِ اللهِ.

Allah ﷻ has servants whom He has created for the needs of people. People rush to them for the fulfilments of their needs. They are the ones who are safeguarded from His punishment.[3]

---

[1] Narrated by Muslim in *al-Ṣaḥīḥ*, 4:2074 §2699; and al-Tirmidhī in *al-Jāmiʿ al-Ṣaḥīḥ*, 4:34 §1425.

[2] Narrated by al-Bukhārī in *al-Tārīkh al-kabīr*, 6:404 §2793; al-Ṭabarānī in *al-Muʿjam al-kabīr*, 5:118 §4802; and al-Daylamī in *Musnad al-Firdaws*, 5:91 §7560.

[3] Narrated by al-Ṭabarānī in *al-Muʿjam al-kabīr*, 2:358 §13,334; al-Quḍāʿī in *Musnad al-shihāb*, 2:117 §1007-1008; and al-Mundhirī in *al-Targhīb wa al-tarhīb*, 3:262 §3966.

Allah ﷻ loves that His servants assist one another that He has appointed some people to be responsible for the assistance of others.

5. ʿAbd Allāh b. ʿUmar and Abū Hurayra both narrate that the Holy Prophet ﷺ said:

مَنْ مَشَى فِي حَاجَةِ أَخِيهِ الْـمُسْلِمِ حَتَّى يُتِمَّهَا لَهُ؛ أَظَلَّهُ اللهُ بِخَمْسَةِ آلَافٍ (وَفِي رِوَايَةٍ: بِخَمْسَةٍ وَسَبْعِينَ أَلْفَ) مَلَكٍ يَدْعُونَ لَهُ وَيُصَلُّونَ عَلَيْهِ، إِنْ كَانَ صَبَاحًا حَتَّى يُمْسِيَ، وَإِنْ كَانَ مَسَاءً حَتَّى يُصْبِحَ، لا يَرْفَعُ قَدَمًا إِلا كُتِبَ لَهُ بِهَا حَسَنَةٌ، وَلا يَضَعُ قَدَمًا إِلا حُطَّتْ عَنْهُ بِهَا خَطِيئَةٌ.

> If someone sets out to carry out a job for his brother and completes it, Allah ﷻ appoints fifty thousand (according to another narration: it is seventy-five thousand) angels to look over him, who pray for him; if it is day (they continue to pray for him) till the night, and if it is night (they continue to pray for him) till the morning. He does not raise his foot to take a step except that a good deed is written for him; and he does not place his foot on the ground, except that a sin is wiped out for him.[1]

These hadiths point out how great a deal it is to assist others. The reason why selfishness, chaos and uncertainty are common in our societies is because people no longer consider the pain of others as their own as they do not share their pains and sorrow. Selfishness is on the increase with people not keeping in touch with their neighbours let alone share their pains and sorrow. Therefore, in order to

---

[1] Narrated by al-Bayhaqī in *Shuʿab al-īmān*, 6:119 §7669; and al-Ṭabarānī in *al-Muʿjam al-awsaṭ*, 4:347 §4396.

set up a truly Islamic society, it is vital for the true Islamic values to be implemented at the individual and collective level where people help each other financially, practically and emotionally.

Q.118. WHAT VIRTUES ARE MENTIONED IN THE HADITHS FOR LENDING A *QARḌ ḤASANA* TO THE NEEDY?

A: Islam motivates and encourages people to provide financial support to the needy so that their needs can be met. However, if someone is not financially able to do this then *qarḍ ḥasana* should be given. Guidelines have been provided to the lender so he or she does not exert too much pressure on the debtor, so that the matter is dealt with in any easy and hassle free manner.

1. Ḥudhayfa narrates that the Holy Prophet ﷺ said:

تَلَقَّتِ الْـمَلاَئِكَةُ رُوحَ رَجُلٍ مِمَّنْ كَانَ قَبْلَكُمْ فَقَالُوا: أَعَمِلْتَ مِنَ الْخَيْرِ شَيْئًا. قَالَ لاَ. قَالُوا تَذَكَّرْ. قَالَ كُنْتُ أُدَايِنُ النَّاسَ فَآمُرُ فِتْيَانِي أَنْ يُنْظِرُوا الْـمُعْسِرَ وَيَتَجَوَّزُوا عَنِ الْـمُوسِرِ. قَالَ ﷺ: قَالَ اللهُ تَعَالَى تَجَوَّزُوا عَنْهُ.

The angels took away the soul of a person who had lived among people who were before you. They (the angels) said: "Did you do anything good?" He said: "No." They said: "Try to recall." He said: "I used to lend to people and order my servants to give respite to one in straitened circumstances and give allowance to the solvent."

Allah ﷻ said (to the angels): "You should ignore (his failing)."[1]

2. Abū Hurayra narrates that the Holy Prophet ﷺ said:

كَانَ تَاجِرٌ يُدَايِنُ النَّاسَ، فَإِذَا رَأَى مُعْسِرًا قَالَ لِفِتْيَانِهِ: تَجَاوَزُوا عَنْهُ، لَعَلَّ اللهَ أَنْ يَتَجَاوَزَ عَنَّا، فَتَجَاوَزَ اللهُ عَنْهُ.

There was a merchant who used to lend the people, and whenever his debtor was in straitened circumstances, he would say to his employees, "Forgive him so that Allah ﷻ may forgive us." So, Allah forgave him.[2]

This hadith has been mentioned in greater detail in *Sunan al-Nasāʾī*:

إِنَّ رَجُلاً لَمْ يَعْمَلْ خَيْرًا قَطُّ وَكَانَ يُدَايِنُ النَّاسَ فَيَقُولُ لِرَسُولِهِ خُذْ مَا تَيَسَّرَ وَاتْرُكْ مَا عَسُرَ وَتَجَاوَزْ لَعَلَّ اللهَ تَعَالَى أَنْ يَتَجَاوَزَ عَنَّا. فَلَمَّا هَلَكَ قَالَ ﷻ لَهُ: هَلْ عَمِلْتَ خَيْرًا قَطُّ. قَالَ: لاَ إِلَّا أَنَّهُ كَانَ لِي غُلَامٌ وَكُنْتُ أُدَايِنُ النَّاسَ فَإِذَا بَعَثْتُهُ لِيَتَقَاضَى قُلْتُ لَهُ خُذْ مَا تَيَسَّرَ وَاتْرُكْ مَا عَسُرَ وَتَجَاوَزْ لَعَلَّ اللهَ يَتَجَاوَزُ عَنَّا. قَالَ اللهُ تَعَالَى قَدْ تَجَاوَزْتُ عَنْكَ.

There was a man who never did any good deed, but he used to lend to people and he would say to this messenger: "Take what can be paid easily and leave what is difficult, let them off, and perhaps Allah will forgive us." When the man

---

[1] Narrated by al-Bukhārī in *al-Ṣaḥīḥ*, 2:731 §1971; and Muslim in *al-Ṣaḥīḥ*, 3:1194 §1560.

[2] Narrated by al-Bukhārī in *al-Ṣaḥīḥ*, 2:731 §1972; and Muslim in *al-Ṣaḥīḥ*, 3:1196 §1562.

> died, Allah ﷻ said to him: "Did you ever do any good did?" He said: "No, but I had a slave and I used to lend to people. When I sent him to collect the debts I said to him: 'Take what can he paid easily and leave what is difficult; let them off, and perhaps Allah will let us off.'' Allah ﷻ said: "I have let you off."[1]

Allah ﷻ forgave His servant for writing off the loans he gave to the poor and needy. This was because he was doing something which was benefiting creation.

3. It is mentioned in *Ṣaḥīḥ Muslim* that Abū Qatāda requested that a debtor return his loan. Subsequently the debtor hid from Abū Qatāda, but when they met he said, 'I am a poor person and I cannot return the loan right now.' Abū Qatāda replied, 'By Allah, is this true?' He replied, 'Yes, by Allah.' Then Abū Qatāda said that he heard the Holy Prophet ﷺ say:

مَنْ سَرَّهُ أَنْ يُنْجِيَهُ اللهُ مِنْ كُرَبِ يَوْمِ الْقِيَامَةِ فَلْيُنَفِّسْ عَنْ مُعْسِرٍ أَوْ يَضَعْ عَنْهُ.

> Whoever wishes that Allah ﷻ should alleviate his difficulties on the Day of Judgement, let him give ease to the borrower who is in financial difficulty or write off his debts.[2]

4. ʿAbd Allāh b. ʿUmar narrates that the Holy Prophet ﷺ said:

---

[1] Narrated by Aḥmad b. Ḥanbal in *al-Musnad*, 2:361 §8715; al-Nasāʾī in *al-Sunan*, 7:381 §4694; Ibn Ḥibbān in *al-Ṣaḥīḥ*, 11:422 §5403; and al-Ḥākim in *al-Mustadrak*, 2:33 §2223.
[2] Narrated by Muslim in *al-Ṣaḥīḥ*, 3:1196 §1563.

مَنْ أَرَادَ أَنْ تُسْتَجَابَ دَعْوَتُهُ وَأَنْ تُكْشَفَ كُرْبَتُهُ فَلْيُفَرِّجْ عَنْ مُعْسِرٍ.

> Whoever wants that his supplications be accepted and his difficulties removed let him alleviate the financial constraints of a poor person (who is in debt).[1]

There are many ways in which a poor indebted person can have his difficulties alleviated. Either the lender can write off the loan or a wealthy person can repay the debts on his behalf. Both cases results in spending in the path of Allah by which the nearness of Allah ﷻ will be attained.

Q.119. What consequences have borrowers been warned of?

A: Just as giving out loans has been encouraged and the reward has been promised for those who make it easy for their debtors who are in financial difficulty to pay back their loans, in the same way those who do not repay their debts have been warned of torment and chastisement.

1. ᶜAbd Allāh b. ᶜAmr b. al-ᶜĀṣ narrates that the Holy Prophet ﷺ said:

يُغْفَرُ لِلشَّهِيدِ كُلُّ ذَنْبٍ إِلَّا الدَّيْنَ.

> A martyr will have every sin forgiven except for (unpaid) debts.[2]

2. ᶜAbd Allāh b. ᶜAmr also narrates that the Holy Prophet ﷺ said:

---

[1] Narrated by Aḥmad b. Ḥanbal in *al-Musnad*, 2:23 §4749.

[2] Narrated by Muslim in *al-Ṣaḥīḥ*, 3:1502 §1886; Aḥmad b. Ḥanbal in *al-Musnad*, 2:220 §7051; and al-Tirmidhī in *al-Jāmiᶜ al-Ṣaḥīḥ*, 4:175 §1640.

إِنَّ الدَّيْنَ يُقْضَى مِنْ صَاحِبِهِ يَوْمَ الْقِيَامَةِ.

On the Day of Judgement (outstanding) debts will be adjudicated.[1]

3. Samra narrates that the Holy Prophet ﷺ said:

عَلَى الْيَدِ مَا أَخَذَتْ حَتَّى تُؤَدِّيَ.

Every person is liable for what he takes until it is repaid.[2]

Repaying debts is the right of Allah's servants which is known as *ḥuqūq al-ʿibād*. If someone does not fulfill the rights of others, Allah ﷻ will not forgive the offence. Therefore, it is imperative that one repays his or her debts as soon as possible, because one does not know when death will strike, and whether or not the debt owed will be repaid. Therefore paying back debts should be the first priority.

Q.120. What is *ṣadaqa al-fiṭr*?

A: *Ṣadaqa al-fiṭr* is a type of charity which was ordained by the Holy Prophet ﷺ in the same year in which the fast of *Ramaḍān* was obligated. It was made obligatory before the zakah. *Ṣadaqa al-fiṭr* is given to the poor and needy. It is vital for every wealthy person to pay this so that the poor and needy can also enjoy the ʿ*Īd* celebration. Other than this the *ṣadaqa al-fiṭr* is a means of purifying the fasting person from useless and obscene acts.

---

[1] Narrated by Ibn Mājah in *al-Sunan*, 2:814 §2435; ʿAbd b. Ḥumayd in *al-Musnad*, 1:138 §349; and Isḥāq b. Rāhawayh in *al-Musnad*, 2:484 §1064.

[2] Narrated by al-Tirmidhī in *al-Jāmiʿ al-Ṣaḥīḥ*, 3:566 §1266; Abū Dāwūd in *al-Sunan*, 2:318 §3561; and Ibn Mājah in *al-Sunan*, 2:802 §2400.

ʿAbd Allāh b. ʿAbbās narrates that the Holy Prophet ﷺ said:

فَرَضَ رَسُولُ اللهِ زَكَاةَ الْفِطْرِ طُهْرَةً لِلصَّائِمِ مِنَ اللَّغْوِ وَالرَّفَثِ وَطُعْمَةً لِلْمَسَاكِينِ.

The Messenger of Allah ﷺ obligated the *zakāt al-fiṭr* so that it is a source of purification for the fasting person from useless and obscene acts and a provision for the poor.[1]

Q.121. Who must pay *ṣadaqa al-fiṭr*?

A: *Ṣadaqa al-fiṭr* is *wājib* on all Muslims. ʿAbd Allāh b. ʿUmar narrates that the Holy Prophet ﷺ said:

فَرَضَ رَسُولُ اللهِ زَكَاةَ الْفِطْرِ صَاعًا مِنْ تَـمْرٍ أَوْ صَاعًا مِنْ شَعِيرٍ عَلَى الْعَبْدِ وَالْـحُرِّ وَالذَّكَرِ وَالْأُنْثَى وَالصَّغِيرِ وَالْكَبِيرِ مِنَ الْـمُسْلِمِينَ.

The Messenger of Allah ﷺ obligated the *zakāt al-fiṭr* amounting to one *ṣāʿ* of dates or one *ṣāʿ* of barley upon every slave and free person, male and female, young and old from the Muslims (who can afford it).[2]

Abū Hurayra narrates that the Holy Prophet ﷺ said:

---

[1] Narrated by Abū Dāwūd in *al-Sunan*, 2:111 §1609; Ibn Mājah in *al-Sunan*, 1:585 §1827; al-Dārquṭnī in *al-Sunan*, 2:138; al-Ḥākim in *al-Mustadrak*, 1:568 §1488; and al-Daylamī in *Musnad al-Firdaws*, 2:296 §3348.

[2] Narrated by al-Bukhārī in *al-Ṣaḥīḥ*, 2:547 §1432; al-Nasāʾī in *al-Sunan*, 5:48 §2504; and al-Bayhaqī in *al-Sunan al-kubrā*, 4:162 §7477.

لَا صَدَقَةَ إِلَّا عَنْ ظَهْرِ غِنًى.

There is no *ṣadaqa al-fiṭr* except on a wealthy person.[1]

According to the Shariah, a wealthy person is someone upon whom zakah is obligatory, or if the zakah is not obligatory then at least the person possesses the basic needs (such as a home, furniture, appliances, clothes, etc.) the value of which would make the zakah obligatory on him. Regardless whether one possesses trade goods or not, or a lunar year passes on one's possession, the *ṣadaqa al-fiṭr* will be obligatory.

Q.122. WHEN MUST *ṢADAQA AL-FIṬR* BE PAID?

A: The ruling on paying *ṣadaqa al-fiṭr* is that it must be paid before the *ᶜĪd* prayer so that the poor can also partake in the *ᶜĪd* celebration. The Holy Prophet ﷺ instructed that people should pay the *ṣadaqa al-fiṭr* before leaving to offer the *ᶜĪd* prayer.[2] However if someone was unable to pay it before the *ᶜĪd* prayer due to an unavoidable reason then it will also be accepted but the best time to give it was missed as the purpose of *ṣadaqa al-fiṭr* is to prevent the poor from having to beg.

أُغْنُوهُمْ فِي هَذَا الْيَومِ.

Free the poor (from having to beg) on this day.[3]

The more the *ṣadaqa al-fiṭr* is delayed, the more the purpose for which it is given will not be fulfilled. So it is best to pay *ṣadaqa al-fiṭr* before the last ten days of the

---

[1] Narrated by Aḥmad b. Ḥanbal in *al-Musnad*, 2:230 §7155.
[2] Narrated by al-Bukhārī in *al-Ṣaḥīḥ*, 2:547 §1432 and 2:548 §1438.
[3] Narrated by al-Dārquṭnī in *al-Sunan*, 2:152 §67.

month of *Ramaḍān* so that the poor can also enjoy *ᶜĪd* like everyone else.

Q.123. WHAT ARE THE BENEFITS OF *ṢADAQA AL-FIṬR*?

A: *Ṣadaqa al-fiṭr* has the following benefits:

1. Paying it earns the reward for acting upon a ruling of the Shariah.
2. It is a means of overcoming the shortfalls of fasting and purifying one's fasts.
3. It is a demonstration of altruism where the needs of the poor are fulfilled so that they may partake in the *ᶜĪd* celebration.

Q.124. WHAT ARE THE VIRTUES OF GIVING CHARITY IN *RAMAḌĀN*?

A: Charity is that wealth which is given to the poor in order to gain the pleasure of Allah. There is great reward in spending in Allah's path and there are many benefits in this world and the life hereafter. The virtues and benefits of giving charity in *Ramaḍān* are mentioned in the books of hadiths.

1. Anas b. Mālik narrates that the Holy Prophet ﷺ was asked, 'which charity is the best?', and the Holy Prophet ﷺ replied:

صَدَقَةٌ فِي رَمَضَانَ.

Charity in the month of *Ramaḍān*.[1]

2. ᶜAbd Allāh b. ᶜAbbās narrates:

---

[1] Narrated by al-Tirmidhī in *al-Jāmiᶜ al-Ṣaḥīḥ*, 2:43 §663; and al-Bayhaqī in *al-Sunan al-kubrā*, 4:305 §8300.

كَانَ النَّبِيُّ ﷺ أَجْوَدَ النَّاسِ بِالْخَيْرِ، وَكَانَ أَجْوَدُ مَا يَكُونُ فِي رَمَضَانَ، حِينَ يَلْقَاهُ جِبْرِيلُ، وَكَانَ جِبْرِيلُ عليه السلام يَلْقَاهُ كُلَّ لَيْلَةٍ فِي رَمَضَانَ حَتَّى يَنْسَلِخَ، يَعْرِضُ عَلَيْهِ النَّبِيُّ ﷺ الْقُرْآنَ، فَإِذَا لَقِيَهُ جِبْرِيلُ عليه السلام كَانَ أَجْوَدَ بِالْخَيْرِ مِنَ الرِّيحِ الْمُرْسَلَةِ.

The Prophet ﷺ was the most generous amongst the people, and he used to be more so in the month of *Ramaḍān* when Jibrīl ﷺ visited him, and Jibrīl ﷺ used to meet him on every night of *Ramaḍān* till the end of the month. The Prophet ﷺ used to recite the Qurʾān to Jibrīl ﷺ, and when Jibrīl ﷺ met him, he used to be more generous than a fast wind.[1]

Q.125. Who are the most deserving to receive charity?

A: The people who are the most deserving to receive charity are one's needy relatives, such as one's brother, sister, nephew, niece, uncle, aunty, father-in-law, mother-in-law, son-in-law, daughter-in-law, and so on. Giving charity to them is highly rewarding. After that, it is better to give it to one's neighbours or the people of one's locality to those who are more deserving. Then those people should be given charity by which the religion will be benefitted such as students and researchers, etc.

Ṭāriq al-Muḥāribī narrates that when he came to Medina, the Holy Prophet ﷺ was delivering a sermon:

يَدُ الْمُعْطِي الْعُلْيَا، وَابْدَأْ بِمَنْ تَعُولُ: أُمَّكَ وَأَبَاكَ وَأُخْتَكَ وَأَخَاكَ ثُمَّ أَدْنَاكَ أَدْنَاكَ.

---

[1] Narrated by al-Bukhārī in *al-Ṣaḥīḥ*, 2:672 §1803.

> The giving hand is the higher hand, and begin by giving charity to those for who you are responsible providing for, such as your mother, father, sister, and brother; and then to your closest relationship.[1]

Q.126. Can an insignificant thing be given as charity?

A: Yes, a small and insignificant thing can be given as charity as long as it is earned lawfully.

1. Abū Hurayra narrates that the Holy Prophet ﷺ said:

> مَنْ تَصَدَّقَ بِعَدْلِ تَمْرَةٍ مِنْ كَسْبٍ طَيِّبٍ، وَلَا يَقْبَلُ اللهُ إِلاَّ الطَّيِّبَ، وَإِنَّ اللهَ يَتَقَبَّلُهَا بِيَمِينِهِ، ثُمَّ يُرَبِّيهَا لِصَاحِبِهِ كَمَا يُرَبِّي أَحَدُكُمْ فَلُوَّهُ حَتَّى تَكُونَ مِثْلَ الْجَبَلِ.

> If one donates one date-fruit from one's money which is earned honestly, and Allah ﷻ only accepts honest earnings, Allah ﷻ takes it in His right (hand) and then enlarges its reward for that person who has given it, as anyone of you brings up his baby horse, so much so that it becomes as big as a mountain.[2]

2. In another narration, Abū Hurayra narrates that the Holy Prophet ﷺ said:

---

[1] Narrated by Aḥmad b. Ḥanbal in *al-Musnad*, 4:64 §163; and al-Nasāʾī in *al-Sunan*, 5:61 §2532.

[2] Narrated by al-Bukhārī in *al-Ṣaḥīḥ*, 2:511 §1344; Muslim in *al-Ṣaḥīḥ*, 2:702 §1014; Aḥmad b. Ḥanbal in *al-Musnad*, 2:331 §8363 and 2:381 §8948; al-Tirmidhī in *al-Jāmiʿ al-Ṣaḥīḥ*, 3:69 §661; al-Nasāʾī in *al-Sunan*, 5:57 §2525; Ibn Mājah in *al-Sunan*, 1:590 §1842; and Mālik in *al-Muwaṭṭaʾ*, 20:995 §1806.

يَا نِسَاءَ الْمُسْلِمَاتِ! لَا تَحْقِرَنَّ جَارَةٌ لِجَارَتِهَا وَلَوْ فِرْسِنَ شَاةٍ.

O Muslim women! Do not consider the gift from your female neighbour as insignificant, even if it is the hooves of a goat.[1]

3. ʿAbd Allāh b. Masʿūd narrates that the Holy Prophet ﷺ said:

لِيَتَّقِ أَحَدُكُمْ وَجْهَهُ النَّارَ، وَلَوْ بِشِقِّ تَمْرَةٍ.

Let one of you save his face from the Hellfire, even if it is by half a date.[2]

Every Muslim should continue to give charity according to their ability and circumstance and the practice of giving charity should not be abandoned due to a lack of wealth and property. Neither should anything given by anyone be deemed as meagre or insulting, because Allah accepts even minor and insignificant good deeds and does not let it go to a waste. The Qurʾān states:

﴿فَمَن يَعْمَلْ مِثْقَالَ ذَرَّةٍ خَيْرًا يَرَهُۥ﴾

Then he who will have done even an atom's weight of good will see it.[3]

Q.127. Can charity be given from unlawful earnings?

A: It is not permissible to give charity from unlawful earnings because Allah ﷻ only accepts charity which is

[1] Narrated by al-Bukhārī in *al-Ṣaḥīḥ*, 2:907 §2427 and 5:2240 §5671; and Muslim in *al-Ṣaḥīḥ*, 2:714 §1030.
[2] Narrated by Aḥmad b. Ḥanbal in *al-Musnad*, 1:388 §3679; and al-Haythamī in *Majmaʿ al-zawāʾid*, 3:105.
[3] Qurʾān 99:7.

given from one's earnings which are lawful. Abū Hurayra narrates that the Holy Prophet ﷺ said:

مَنْ تَصَدَّقَ بِعَدْلِ تَمْرَةٍ مِنْ كَسْبٍ طَيِّبٍ، وَلَا يَقْبَلُ اللهُ إِلاَّ الطَّيِّبَ، وَإِنَّ اللهَ يَتَقَبَّلُهَا بِيَمِينِهِ، ثُمَّ يُرَبِّيهَا لِصَاحِبِهِ كَمَا يُرَبِّي أَحَدُكُمْ فَلُوَّهُ حَتَّى تَكُونَ مِثْلَ الْجَبَلِ.

> If one donates one date-fruit from one's money which is earned honestly—and Allah ﷻ only accepts honest earnings—Allah ﷻ takes it in His right (hand) and then enlarges its reward for that person who has given it, as anyone of you brings up his baby horse, so much so that it becomes as big as a mountain.[1]

Therefore no matter how great a donation is given from the lawful earnings, it will not be faithful. In another hadith whch is narrated by Abū Hurayra:

مَنْ جَمَعَ مَالًا حَرَامًا ثُمَّ تَصَدَّقَ بِهِ، لَمْ يَكُنْ لَهُ فِيهِ أَجْرٌ وَكَانَ إِصْرُهُ عَلَيْهِ.

> Whoever gathers unlawful wealth and then donates it, there is no reward in it for him and its burden will be upon him.[2]

---

[1] Narrated by al-Bukhārī in *al-Ṣaḥīḥ*, 2:511 §1344; Muslim in *al-Ṣaḥīḥ*, 2:702 §1014; Aḥmad b. Ḥanbal in *al-Musnad*, 2:331 §8363 and 2:381 §8948; al-Tirmidhī in *al-Jāmiʿ al-Ṣaḥīḥ*, 3:69 §661; al-Nasāʾī in *al-Sunan*, 5:57 §2525; Ibn Mājah in *al-Sunan*, 1:590 §1842; and al-Mālik in *al-Muwaṭṭaʾ*, 20:995 §1806.

[2] Narrated by Ibn Ḥibbān in *al-Ṣaḥīḥ*, 8:153 §3367.

Q.128. Is it permissible to reclaim charity after having given it?

A: It is not permissible to give charity and then take it back, in fact it is disliked and a deplorable act. ʿUmar b. al-Khaṭṭāb states:

حَمَلْتُ عَلَى فَرَسٍ فِي سَبِيلِ اللهِ، فَأَضَاعَهُ الَّذِي كَانَ عِنْدَهُ، فَأَرَدْتُ أَنْ أَشْتَرِيَهُ، وَظَنَنْتُ أَنَّهُ يَبِيعُهُ بِرُخْصٍ، فَسَأَلْتُ النَّبِيَّ ﷺ فَقَالَ: لاَ تَشْتَرِ وَلاَ تَعُدْ فِي صَدَقَتِكَ، وَإِنْ أَعْطَاكَهُ بِدِرْهَمٍ، فَإِنَّ الْعَائِدَ فِي صَدَقَتِهِ كَالْعَائِدِ فِي قَيْئِهِ.

> Once I gave a horse in Allah's cause but that person did not take care of it. I intended to buy it, as I thought he would sell it at a low price. So, I asked the Prophet ﷺ about it. He said, "Neither buy, nor take back your alms which you have given, even if the seller were willing to sell it for one dirham, for he who takes back his alms is like the one who swallows his own vomit."[1]

Q.129. Can someone inherit their own donation?

A: According to the following hadith, it is permissible to inherit one's charity that one has given previously. Burayda narrates:

بَيْنَا أَنَا جَالِسٌ عِنْدَ رَسُولِ اللهِ ﷺ إِذْ أَتَتْهُ امْرَأَةٌ. فَقَالَتْ: إِنِّي تَصَدَّقْتُ عَلَى أُمِّي بِجَارِيَةٍ وَإِنَّهَا مَاتَتْ. قَالَ: فَقَالَ: وَجَبَ أَجْرُكِ

[1] Narrated by al-Bukhārī in *al-Ṣaḥīḥ*, 2:542 §1419.

وَرَدَّهَا عَلَيْكِ الْـمِيرَاثُ. قَالَتْ: يَا رَسُولَ اللهِ إِنَّهُ كَانَ عَلَيْهَا صَوْمُ شَهْرٍ أَفَأَصُومُ عَنْهَا. قَالَ: صُومِي عَنْهَا. قَالَتْ: إِنَّهَا لَمْ تَحُجَّ قَطُّ أَفَأَحُجُّ عَنْهَا. قَالَ: حُجِّي عَنْهَا.

> When we were sitting with the Messenger of Allah ﷺ, a woman came to him and said: "I had gifted to my mother a maid-servant, and now she (the mother) has died." Thereupon the Holy Prophet ﷺ said: "There is a definite reward for you; and the maid-servant has been returned to you as an inheritance." She again said: "Fasts of a month are due upon her; should I observe them on her behalf?" He ﷺ said: "Observe fasts on her behalf." She said: "She did not perform the Pilgrimage, should I perform it on her behalf?" He ﷺ said: "Perform the Pilgrimage on her behalf."[1]

The majority of the scholars opine that it is permissible for someone to inherit something he or she has previously donated as charity. While others are of the opinion that as the charity was something that was donated for the sake of Allah, so even if it is inherited, it is obligatory to return it.

Q.130. Can *qarḍ ḥasana* be given out from a fund specified for charity?

A: There are two types of charity: obligatory charity, such as zakah, *ṣadaqa al-fiṭr*, vows (*nadhr*), penalty (*kaffāra*), and compensation (*fidya*); and the voluntary charity

---

[1] Narrated by Muslim in *al-Ṣaḥīḥ*, 2:805 §1149; Aḥmad b. Ḥanbal in *al-Musnad*, 5:349 §23,006 and 2:351 §23,021; al-Tirmidhī in *al-Jāmiʿ al-Ṣaḥīḥ*, 3:54 §667; al-Nasāʾī in *al-Sunan al-kubrā*, 4:66-67 §6314-6316; and Ibn Mājah in *al-Sunan*, 2:800 §2394.

which includes all general types of *ṣadaqa*. The fund containing voluntary charity can be used to give *qarḍ ḥasana*, so that the poor and needy can be helped. There is a condition that permission must be received from the donor/s for this.

Q.131. Can charity be given on behalf of the deceased?

A: Yes, it is permissible to give charity on behalf of a deceased. There is consensus amongst the scholars that by giving charity on behalf of the deceased, the deceased person receives reward for it. It is mentioned in the hadiths that if a loan is paid on behalf of someone who passed away, the debt is written off. The same applies to the obligation of performing the Pilgrimage, in the same way that charity is paid on behalf of a deceased. A few hadiths will be related below in this regard.

1. ʿĀʾisha narrates that the Holy Prophet ﷺ said:

مَنْ مَاتَ وَعَلَيْهِ صِيَامٌ صَامَ عَنْهُ وَلِيُّهُ.

Whoever dies and has outstanding fasts, his guardian should fast on his behalf.[1]

2. ʿAbd Allāh b. ʿAbbās narrates that the Holy Prophet ﷺ said:

وَإِنْ كَانَ عَلَيْهِ نَذْرٌ قَضَى عَنْهُ وَلِيُّهُ.

If the deceased made a vow, his guardian should fulfill it on his behalf.[2]

3. ʿĀʾisha narrates that the Holy Prophet ﷺ said:

---

[1] Narrated by al-Bukhārī in *al-Ṣaḥīḥ*, 2:690 §1851; Muslim in *al-Ṣaḥīḥ*, 2:803 §1147; Abū Dāwūd in *al-Sunan*, 3:237 §3311; and al-Nasāʾī in *al-Sunan*, 2:175 §2919.

[2] Narrated by Abū Dāwūd in *al-Sunan*, 2:315 §2400-2401.

أَنَّ رَجُلاً قَالَ لِلنَّبِيِّ ﷺ: إِنَّ أُمِّي افْتُلِتَتْ نَفْسُهَا، وَأَظُنُّهَا لَوْ تَكَلَّمَتْ تَصَدَّقَتْ، فَهَلْ لَهَا أَجْرٌ إِنْ تَصَدَّقْتُ عَنْهَا. قَالَ: نَعَمْ.

A man came to the Holy Prophet ﷺ and said, 'My mother died suddenly and I think that if she was able to speak at the time of her death she would have given charity. If I give charity on her behalf, will she receive reward?' The Holy Prophet ﷺ said, 'Yes.'[1]

4. ʿAbd Allāh b. ʿAbbās narrates that the Holy Prophet ﷺ said:

أَنَّ سَعْدَ بْنَ عُبَادَةَ تُوُفِّيَتْ أُمُّهُ وَهْوَ غَائِبٌ عَنْهَا، فَقَالَ: يَا رَسُولَ اللهِ، إِنَّ أُمِّي تُوُفِّيَتْ وَأَنَا غَائِبٌ عَنْهَا، أَيَنْفَعُهَا شَيْءٌ إِنْ تَصَدَّقْتُ بِهِ عَنْهَا. قَالَ: نَعَمْ. قَالَ: فَإِنِّي أُشْهِدُكَ أَنَّ حَائِطِي الْمِخْرَافَ صَدَقَةٌ عَلَيْهَا.

The mother of Saʿd b. ʿUbāda passed away and he was not there at the time. He asked the Holy Prophet ﷺ, 'O Messenger of Allah, my mother died and I was not there at the time. If I give charity on her behalf, will she receive the reward?' The Holy Prophet ﷺ said, 'Yes.' Saʿd said, 'I make you witness that I donate my orchard, *al-Mikhrāf*, as charity on her behalf.'[2]

---

[1] Narrated by al-Bukhārī in *al-Ṣaḥīḥ*, 1:467 §1322; Muslim in *al-Ṣaḥīḥ*, 3:1254 §1004; Abū Dāwūd in *al-Sunan*, 3:118 §2881; al-Nasāʾī in *al-Sunan*, 6:250 §3649; and Ibn Mājah in *al-Sunan*, 2:906 §2717. Imam Muslim narrates this in the chapter on the reward reaching the deceased.

[2] Narrated by al-Bukhārī in *al-Ṣaḥīḥ*, 3:1013 §2605; Aḥmad b. Ḥanbal in *al-Musnad*, 1:370 §3504; al-Tirmidhī in *al-Jāmiʿ al-Ṣaḥīḥ*,

5. Saʿd b. ʿUbāda narrates that his mother died, so he said, 'O Messenger of Allah, my mother has died, can I give charity on her behalf?' The Holy Prophet ﷺ said, 'Yes.' He asked, 'So which charity is best?' The Holy Prophet ﷺ said, 'Giving water to people.' So he bought a well and donated it to the Muslims. Thus this well was known in Medina as the well of *Āl al-Saʿd*.[1]

6. Abū Hurayra narrates that a man said to the Holy Prophet ﷺ, 'O Messenger of Allah! My father has died and he has left some wealth, but he did not write a will. If I give charity on his behalf will that expiate for his sins?' The Holy Prophet ﷺ said, 'Yes.'[2]

7. ʿAbd Allāh b. ʿAbbās narrates that a woman came to the Holy Prophet ﷺ and said, 'My mother has passed away and a month's fasts are owed by her.' The Holy Prophet ﷺ said, 'Tell me, if she had a debt to pay, will you pay it?' She replied, 'Yes.' So the Holy Prophet ﷺ said, 'Thus, Allah ﷻ is more deserving that you pay off His debt first.'[3]

8. ʿAbd Allāh b. ʿAbbās narrates that a woman asked the Holy Prophet ﷺ, 'My father passed away and he did not perform the Pilgrimage.' The Holy Prophet ﷺ said, 'You perform the Pilgrimage on his behalf.'[4]

3:56 §669; Abū Dāwūd in *al-Sunan*, 3:118 §2882; and al-Nasāʾī in *al-Sunan*, 6:252 §3655.

[1] Narrated by Aḥmad b. Ḥanbal in *al-Musnad*, 5:284 §22,512; Abū Dāwūd in *al-Sunan*, 2:130 §1681; al-Nasāʾī in *al-Sunan*, 6:254-255 §3662-3666; and Ibn Mājah in *al-Sunan*, 2:1214 §3684.

[2] Narrated by Muslim in *al-Ṣaḥīḥ*, 3:1254 §1630; Aḥmad b. Ḥanbal in *al-Musnad*, 2:371 §8828; al-Nasāʾī in *al-Sunan*, 6:251 §3652; and Ibn Mājah in *al-Sunan*, 2:206 §2716.

[3] Narrated by Muslim in *al-Ṣaḥīḥ*, 2:804 §1148; Ibn Ḥibbān in *al-Ṣaḥīḥ*, 8:299 §3530 and 8:335 §3570; and al-Bayhaqī in *al-Sunan al-kubrā*, 4:255 §8012.

[4] Narrated by al-Nasāʾī in *al-Sunan*, 5:116 §2634; and al-Ṭabarānī in *al-Muʿjam al-awsaṭ*, 6:87 §5877 and in *al-Muʿjam al-kabīr*, 18:284 §727.

9. ʿAbd Allāh b. ʿAbbās narrates that a man came to the Holy Prophet ﷺ and said, 'My sister passed away and she did not perform the Pilgrimage, so can I perform it on her behalf?' The Holy Prophet ﷺ said, 'If she had outstanding debt, will you pay if off? So Allah is more worthy to be obeyed.'[1]

10. ʿAbd Allāh b. ʿUmar narrates that the Holy Prophet ﷺ said:

مَنْ مَاتَ وَعَلَيْهِ صِيَامُ شَهْرٍ فَلْيُطْعَمْ عَنْهُ مَكَانَ كُلِّ يَوْمٍ مِسْكِينًا.

Whoever passes away and has a month of fasts to owe, let a destitute person be fed each day on his behalf.[2]

11. ʿAbd Allāh b. ʿAbbās narrates that the Holy Prophet ﷺ said:

إِذَا مَرِضَ الرَّجُلُ فِي رَمَضَانَ ثُمَّ مَاتَ وَلَمْ يَصُمْ أُطْعِمَ عَنْهُ وَلَمْ يَكُنْ عَلَيْهِ قَضَاءٌ وَإِنْ نَذْرٌ قَضَى عَنْهُ وَلِيُّهُ.

If a person falls ill in *Ramaḍān* and then dies, food should be donated on his behalf, and he will not be responsible for the missed fasts. If he vowed to fast, his guardian should fast on his behalf.[3]

12. Ḥansh states that he saw ʿAlī sacrificing two lambs so he asked him, 'What is this?' ʿAlī replied:

---

[1] Narrated by Ibn Ḥibbān in *al-Ṣaḥīḥ*, 9:306 §3993; and Ibn Abī Shayba in *al-Muṣannaf*, 3:339 §14,724.

[2] Narrated by al-Tirmidhī in *al-Jāmiʿ al-Ṣaḥīḥ*, 3:96 §718; Ibn Mājah in *al-Sunan*, 1:558 §1757; and Ibn Khuzayma in *al- Ṣaḥīḥ*, 3:273 §2056.

[3] Narrated by Abū Dāwūd in *al-Sunan*, 2:315 §2401; and al-Bayhaqī in *al-Sunan al-kubrā*, 4:256 §8021.

> The Holy Prophet ﷺ had instructed me to perform a sacrifice on his behalf. So according to that I always perform one sacrifice on behalf of the Holy Prophet ﷺ.[1]

The above mentioned hadiths prove that virtuous and pious deeds can be performed on behalf a deceased person and that they receive this reward.

Q.132. Can a woman give charity from her husband's property?

A: A woman can give charity from her husband's property when there is consent from the husband. If she knows that by donating certain items, the husband will be unhappy about it, then it is not permitted for her to donate such things. If a woman gives charity with the approval of her husband, then she, her husband and any person whom she gives the charity through receives reward.

1. ʿĀʾisha narrates that the Holy Prophet ﷺ said:

إِذَا أَنْفَقَتِ الْـمَرْأَةُ مِنْ طَعَامِ بَيْتِهَا غَيْرَ مُفْسِدَةٍ كَانَ لَهَا أَجْرُهَا بِمَا أَنْفَقَتْ وَلِزَوْجِهَا أَجْرُهُ بِمَا كَسَبَ وَلِلْخَازِنِ مِثْلُ ذَلِكَ لاَ يَنْقُصُ بَعْضُهُمْ أَجْرَ بَعْضٍ شَيْئًا.

> When a woman gives in charity some of the food in her house, without causing any damage, there is reward for her for whatever she has given, and a reward for her husband for what he earned. The same applies to the trustee. In no respect does the one diminish the reward of the other.[2]

---

[1] Narrated by Aḥmad b. Ḥanbal in *al-Musnad*, 2:702 §1200; Abū Dāwūd in *al-Sunan*, 3:94 §2790; Abū Yaʿlā in *al-Musnad*, 1:355 §459; and al-Ḥākim in *al-Musnad*, 4:255 §7556.

[2] Narrated by Muslim in *al-Ṣaḥīḥ*, 2:710 §1024.

2. In another narration, ʿĀʾisha narrates that the Holy Prophet ﷺ said:

إِذَا تَصَدَّقَتِ الْـمَرْأَةُ مِنْ بَيْتِ زَوْجِهَا كَانَ لَهَا بِهِ أَجْرٌ وَلِلزَّوْجِ مِثْلُ ذَلِكَ وَلِلْخَازِنِ مِثْلُ ذَلِكَ وَلاَ يَنْقُصُ كُلُّ وَاحِدٍ مِنْهُمْ مِنْ أَجْرِ صَاحِبِهِ شَيْئًا لَهُ بِمَا كَسَبَ وَلَهَا بِمَا أَنْفَقَتْ.

> When a woman gives in charity from her husband's house, she will get the reward for it, and for her husband is the same as that, and for the trustee is the same as that. The reward of each of them will not be decreased at all by the reward of the other, for him is what he earned, and for her is what she spent.[1]

If however, the husband is very wealthy and affluent but is tight fisted and miserly, the woman can spend his money without his permission.

Q.133. Can a woman donate her personal property without her husband's permission?

A: Yes, a woman can give her personal property away in charity without the permission of her husband.

Q.134. What is the ruling on begging?

A: In Islam begging is a disliked and deplorable act. It has been highly condemned.

1. ʿĀʾidh b. ʿAmr narrates:

---

[1] Narrated by Aḥmad b. Ḥanbal in *al-Musnad*, 6:99 §24,724; al-Tirmidhī in *al-Jāmiʿ al-Ṣaḥīḥ*, 3:58 §671; al-Nasāʾī in *al-Sunan*, 5:65 §2539; and al-Bayhaqī in *al-Sunan al-kubrā*, 5:379 §9196.

أَنَّ رَجُلاً أَتَى النَّـ ـِ ﷺ فَسَأَلَهُ فَأَعْطَاهُ فَلَمَّا وَضَعَ رِجْلَهُ عَلَى أُسْكُفَّةِ الْبَابِ. قَالَ رَسُولُ ا ِ ﷺ: لَوْ تَعْلَمُونَ مَا فِي الْـمَسْأَلَةِ مَا مَشَى أَحَدٌ إِلَى أَحَدٍ يَسْأَلُهُ شَيْئًا.

A man came to the Holy Prophet ﷺ and asked him and he gave him, and when he placed his foot on the threshold the Messenger of Allah ﷺ said, "If you knew how bad begging is, no one would go to anyone else and ask him for anything."[1]

2. ʿĀʾidh b. ʿAmr narrates:

مَا يَزَالُ الرَّجُلُ يَسْأَلُ النَّاسَ حَتَّى يَأْتِيَ يَوْمَ الْقِيَامَةِ لَيْسَ فِي وَجْهِهِ مُزْعَةُ لَحْمٍ.

A man keeps on asking others for something till he comes on the Day of Judgement without any piece of flesh on his face.[2]

3. Samra b. Jundub narrates that the Holy Prophet ﷺ said:

إِنَّ الْـمَسْأَلَةَ كَدٌّ يَكُدُّ بِهَا الرَّجُلُ وَجْهَهُ إِلاَّ أَنْ يَسْأَلَ الرَّجُلُ سُلْطَانًا أَوْ فِي أَمْرٍ لاَ بُدَّ مِنْهُ.

Asking is a labour that toils on a man's face, except if a man asks for something from the ruler,

---

[1] Narrated by al-Nasāʾī in *al-Sunan*, 5:94 §2586; al-Shaybānī in *al-Āḥād wa al-mathānī*, 2:328 §1094; and al-Maqdisī in *al-Aḥādīth al-mukhtāra*, 8:235 §280.

[2] Narrated by al-Bukhārī in *al-Ṣaḥīḥ*, 2:536 §1405.

or he asks for something that he cannot do without.[1]

4. Abū Hurayra narrates that the Holy Prophet ﷺ said:

مَنْ سَأَلَ النَّاسَ أَمْوَالَهُمْ تَكَثُّرًا فَإِنَّمَا يَسْأَلُ جَمْرَ جَهَنَّمَ فَلْيَسْتَقِلَّ مِنْهُ أَوْ لِيُكْثِرْ.

Whoever begs from people so as to accumulate more riches, he is asking for a live coal from hell, so let him ask for a lot or a little.[2]

Begging is such a deplorable act because it encourages people not to work, in turn it leads to a society of work shy people. Islam is a religion that encourages its followers to continually remain active and to work. There is no room in Islam for people to sit at home and expect that Allah ﷻ will provide for them or that others will give them financial support. Allah ﷻ has also instructed His Beloved Prophet ﷺ that the affairs of the world and the *Umma* must be dealt with first before resorting to worship.

It is stated in the Qurʾān:

﴿فَإِذَا فَرَغْتَ فَٱنصَبْ ۝٧ وَإِلَىٰ رَبِّكَ فَٱرْغَب﴾

So when you are free (from educating the Umma (Community), preaching the Din (Religion) and fighting, and fulfilling your responsibilities), then

[1] Narrated by Aḥmad b. Ḥanbal in *al-Musnad*, 5:10 §20,118; al-Tirmidhī in *al-Jāmiᶜ al-Ṣaḥīḥ*, 3:65 §681; al-Nasāʾī in *al-Sunan*, 5:100 §2600; Ibn Ḥibbān in *al-Ṣaḥīḥ*, 8:181 §3386; and al-Ṭabarānī in *al-Muᶜjam al-kabīr*, 7:163 §6769.

[2] Narrated by Ibn Mājah in *al-Sunan*, 1:589 §1838.

strive hard (in remembrance and the worship of your Lord), and turn to your Lord earnestly.[1]

5. Abū Hurayra narrates that the Holy Prophet ﷺ said:

وَالَّذِي نَفْسِي بِيَدِهِ لأَنْ يَأْخُذَ أَحَدُكُمْ حَبْلَهُ فَيَحْتَطِبَ عَلَى ظَهْرِهِ
خَيْرٌ لَهُ مِنْ أَنْ يَأْتِيَ رَجُلاً، فَيَسْأَلَهُ، أَعْطَاهُ أَوْ مَنَعَهُ.

By Him in Whose Hand my life is, it is better for anyone of you to take a rope and cut the wood (from the forest) and carry it over his back and sell it (as a means of earning his living) rather than to ask a person for something and that person may give him or not.[2]

6. This is the reason why the Companions used to be very cautious before asking anyone for anything. Abū Saʿīd al-Khudrī narrates:

سَرَّحَتْنِي أُمِّي إِلَى رَسُولِ ﷺ فَأَتَيْتُهُ فَقَعَدْتُ، فَاسْتَقْبَلَنِي وَقَالَ:
مَنِ اسْتَغْنَى أَغْنَاهُ اللهُ. وَمَنِ اسْتَعَفَّ أَعَفَّهُ اللهُ وَمَنِ اسْتَكْفَ كَفَاهُ
اللهُ وَمَنْ سَأَلَ وَلَهُ قِيمَةُ أُوقِيَّةٍ فَقَدْ أَلْحَفَ. فَقُلْتُ: نَاقَتِي الْيَاقُوتَةُ
خَيْرٌ مِنْ أُوقِيَّةٍ فَرَجَعْتُ وَلَمْ أَسْأَلْهُ.

My mother sent me to the Messenger of Allah (to request something), so I went there and sat down. The Holy Prophet ﷺ turned towards me and said, "Whoever is free from relying on others, Allah ﷻ will make him free of need. Whoever desists from begging, Allah ﷻ will ensure that he is not dependent on others. Whoever is content with having a little, Allah ﷻ will suffice Him. And

[1] Qurʾān 94:7-8.
[2] Narrated by al-Bukhārī in *al-Ṣaḥīḥ*, 2:535 §1401.

> whoever begs and he has assets equivalent to one ʾ*ūqiya* (40 dirhams), he has begged persistently." I said to myself, 'I have a camel named *Yāqūta* and it is more valuable than one ʾ*ūqiya*.' I came back and did not request anything from the Holy Prophet ﷺ.[1]

The above mentioned hadiths make it clear how disliked the act of begging is in Islam. The permission to ask others for anything is only given in cases of dire need. In fact, it would be better to say that it is only permitted to beg in situations of life and death.

7. Anas b. Mālik narrates that the Holy Prophet ﷺ said:

> إِنَّ الْـمَسْأَلَةَ لَا تَحِلُّ إِلَّا لِثَلَاثَةٍ: لِذِي فَقْرٍ مُدْقِعٍ، أَوْ لِذِي غُرْمٍ مُفْظِعٍ، أَوْ لِذِي دَمٍ مُوجِعٍ.

> It is not permitted for anyone to beg except in three situations: a destitute who is in dire poverty; a person heavily in debt; and the one who has to pay blood money.[2]

8. ʿUbayd Allāh b. ʿAdī b. Khiyār narrates that the Holy Prophet ﷺ said:

> أَخْبَرَنِي رَجُلَانِ أَنَّهُمَا أَتَيَا النَّبِيَّ ﷺ وَهُوَ فِي حَجَّةِ الْوَدَاعِ، وَهُوَ يُقَسِّمُ الصَّدَقَةَ فَسَأَلَاهُ مِنْهَا، فَرَفَعَ فِينَا النَّظَرَ، وَخَفَضَهُ فَرَآنَا

---

[1] Narrated by Aḥmad b. Ḥanbal in *al-Musnad*, 3:7 §11,059; Abū Dāwūd in *al-Sunan*, 2:116 §1628; al-Nasāʾī in *al-Sunan*, 5:98 §2595; al-Dārquṭnī in *al-Sunan*, 2:118 §1; and al-Ṭabarānī in *al-Muʿjam al-kabīr*, 2:150 §1630.

[2] Narrated by Aḥmad b. Ḥanbal in *al-Musnad*, 3:126 §12,300; Abū Dāwūd in *al-Sunan*, 2:120 §1641; Ibn Mājah in *al-Sunan*, 2:740 §2198; and al-Ṭayālasī in *al-Musnad*, 1:285 §2145.

جَلْدَيْنِ، فَقَالَ: إِنْ شِئْتُمَا أَعْطَيْتُكُمَا وَلَا حَظَّ فِيهَا لِغَنِيٍّ وَلَا لِقَوِيٍّ مُكْتَسِبٍ.

Two men came to the Holy Prophet ﷺ whilst he was performing the Farewell Pilgrimage; he was distributing charity. They asked for something from it so the Holy Prophet ﷺ raised his eyes and looked and then lowered them again. The Holy Prophet ﷺ said that we were both strong and healthy. The Holy Prophet ﷺ said, "If you want I can give you something from it, but those who are affluent or are able to earn a living, they have no right over it."[1]

The habit of begging or always asking others for financial support not only leads individuals and nations to become economically stagnant, but it will lead to the nation becoming negatively affected both psychologically and spiritually.

Q.135. What is the virtue of not begging despite being needy?

A: If someone is needy, he or she should avoid begging as much as possible as there are many virtues listed in the hadiths for avoiding begging.

1. ʿAbd Allāh b. ʿAmr narrates that the Holy Prophet ﷺ said:

[1] Narrated by Aḥmad b. Ḥanbal in *al-Musnad*, 4:224 §18,001; Abū Dāwūd in *al-Sunan*, 2:118 §1633; al-Nasāʾī in *al-Sunan*, 5:99 §2598; ʿAbd al-Razzāq in *al-Muṣannaf*, 4:109 §7154; Ibn Abī Shayba in *al-Muṣannaf*, 2:424 §10,666; al-Dārquṭnī in *al-Sunan*, 2:119 §7; and al-Ṭabarānī in *al-Muʿjam al-awsaṭ*, 3:137 §2722.

أَنَّ رَسُولَ ا ﷺ قَالَ وَهُوَ عَلَى الْـمِنْبَرِ، وَذَكَرَ الصَّدَقَةَ وَالتَّعَفُّفَ وَالْـمَسْأَلَةَ: الْيَدُ الْعُلْيَا خَيْرٌ مِنَ الْيَدِ السُّفْلَى، فَالْيَدُ الْعُلْيَا هِيَ الْـمُنْفِقَةُ، وَالسُّفْلَى هِيَ السَّائِلَةُ.

I heard Allah's Messenger ﷺ while he was on the pulpit speaking about charity, to abstain from asking others for some financial help and about begging others, saying, "The upper hand is better than the lower hand. The upper hand is that of the giver and the lower (hand) is that of the beggar."[1]

2. Thawbān narrates that the Holy Prophet ﷺ said, "Whoever guarantees to me that he will never ask people for things, I will guarantee him Paradise." Thawbān said, "I give you a guarantee on this." This Thawbān never used to ask anyone for anything.[2]

3. Abū Saʿīd al-Khudrī narrates:

أَنَّ نَاسًا مِنَ الأَنْصَارِ سَأَلُوا رَسُولَ ا ﷺ فَأَعْطَاهُمْ، ثُمَّ سَأَلُوهُ فَأَعْطَاهُمْ، حَتَّى نَفِدَ مَا عِنْدَهُ فَقَالَ: مَا يَكُونُ عِنْدِي مِنْ خَيْرٍ فَلَنْ أَدَّخِرَهُ عَنْكُمْ، وَمَنْ يَسْتَعْفِفْ يُعِفَّهُ اللهُ، وَمَنْ يَسْتَغْنِ يُغْنِهِ اللهُ، وَمَنْ يَتَصَبَّرْ يُصَبِّرْهُ اللهُ، وَمَا أُعْطِيَ أَحَدٌ عَطَاءً خَيْرًا وَأَوْسَعَ مِنَ الصَّبْرِ.

---

[1] Narrated by al-Bukhārī in *al-Ṣaḥīḥ*, 2:519 §1362; Muslim in *al-Ṣaḥīḥ*, 2:717 §1033; Aḥmad b. Ḥanbal in *al-Musnad*, 2:67 §5344; Abū Dāwūd in *al-Sunan*, 2:122 §1648; al-Nasāʾī in *al-Sunan*, 5:61 §2533; and al-Mālik in *al-Muwaṭṭaʾ*, 2:998 §1813.

[2] Narrated by Abū Dāwūd in *al-Sunan*, 2:42 §1643; and al-Nasāʾī in *al-Sunan*, 5:96 §2590.

> Someone from the Anṣār asked for something from Allah's Messenger ﷺ and he gave them. They again asked him for (something) and he again gave them. And then they asked him and he gave them again till all that was with him finished. And then he said, "If I had anything. I would not keep it away from you. Whoever abstains from asking others, Allah ﷻ will make him contented, and whoever tries to make himself self-sufficient, Allah ﷻ will make him self-sufficient. And whoever remains patient, Allah ﷻ will make him patient. Nobody can be given a blessing better and greater than patience."[1]

Q.136. What is the ruling on taking charity without asking for it?

A: It is permitted to take charity without having asked for it. ʿUmar ؓ narrates that the Holy Prophet ﷺ said to him:

فَمَا جَاءَكَ مِنْ هَذَا الْمَالِ وَأَنْتَ غَيْرُ مُشْرِفٍ وَلَا سَائِلٍ فَخُذْهُ وَمَالَا فَلَا تُتْبِعْهُ نَفْسَكَ.

> Whatever comes to you of this wealth (i.e., charity) and you do not desire it or ask for it, then take it; and if you do not want to take it then your heart should not incline to it.[2]

---

[1] Narrated by al-Bukhārī in *al-Ṣaḥīḥ*, 2:534-535 §1400; and Muslim in *al-Ṣaḥīḥ*, 2:729 §1053.

[2] Narrated by al-Bukhārī in *al-Ṣaḥīḥ*, 6:2620 §6744; Muslim in *al-Ṣaḥīḥ*, 2:723 §1045; Aḥmad b. Ḥanbal in *al-Musnad*, 1:17 §100 and 1:21 §136; and al-Nasāʾī in *al-Sunan*, 5:104 §2607.

Q.137. What is the ruling on asking in the name of Allah?

A: To ask in the name of Allah is a deplorable and ugly act. Such beggars are not poor or needy, but they ask others in Allah's name due to their lust for accumulating wealth. In reality they are accumulating the flames of the Hellfire. These beggars also trouble Muslims by engaging in emotional blackmail by using Allah's name and then make those who do not donate to them to feel bad about it. Annoying people in this way should be avoided as much as possible. Beggars use the name of Allah a lot, but their practice of begging shows their lack of trust in Allah. They use Allah ﷻ merely as a tool for their begging. This is why there are chapters in the books of hadith that prohibit the use of Allah's name while begging.

Imam Abū Dāwūd relates:

عَنْ جَابِرٍ قَالَ: قَالَ رَسُولُ ﷺ: لَا يُسْأَلُ بِوَجْهِ اللهِ إِلَّا الْجَنَّةُ.

> Jābir narrates that the Messenger of Allah ﷺ said, "Nothing should be sought by the countenance of Allah, except Paradise."[1]

The name of Allah, the Creator and Cherisher of the universe, should not be used for merely gaining a few pennies or a meal, but if something is to be gained with Allah's name, it should be Paradise. This will result in benefit in the life hereafter, whereas worldly benefit will be temporary and will remain in this world and only virtuous deeds will go into the life hereafter.

[1] Narrated by Abū Dāwūd in *al-Sunan*, 2:127 §1671.

Q.138. Is *ṣadaqa al-fiṭr* required on those who do not fast for *Ramaḍān*?

A: Yes, the *ṣadaqa al-fiṭr* is *wājib* for someone who did not fast as fasting is not a condition for *ṣadaqa al-fiṭr*. If someone did not fast due to a legitimate reason such as travelling, illness or decrepitude, or even without a legitimate reason, *ṣadaqa al-fiṭr* still remains *wājib*.

Q.139. Can *ṣadaqa al-fiṭr* be paid before *ᶜĪd* during the month of *Ramaḍān*?

A: Yes, in fact it is much better if the *ṣadaqa al-fiṭr* is paid before the day of *ᶜĪd*, so that the poor and needy can partake in the *ᶜĪd* celebrations. It is established that ᶜAbd Allāh b. ᶜUmar used to pay *ṣadaqa al-fiṭr* one or two days before *ᶜĪd*. Nāfiᶜ states:

كَانُوا يُعْطُونَ قَبْلَ الْـفِطْرِ بِيَوْمٍ أَوْ يَوْمَيْنِ.

> They (Ibn ᶜUmar and other Companions) used to pay *ṣadaqa al-fiṭr* one or two days prior to *ᶜĪd*.[1]

Q.140. Is the *ṣadaqa al-fiṭr* also required by those who are prepubescent?

A: Yes, if the child has money of his own that can be used to pay the *ṣadaqa al-fiṭr*. Otherwise the guardian must pay it on his or her behalf.

Q.141. Who is entitled to receive *ṣadaqa al-fiṭr*?

A: *Ṣadaqa al-fiṭr* is spent upon the same categories who are eligible to receive the zakah. Those who cannot receive the zakah, they also cannot receive the *ṣadaqa al-*

---

[1] Narrated by al-Bukhārī in *al-Ṣaḥīḥ*, 2:549 §1440.

fiṭr. It is better to give preference to the poor and needy because the Holy Prophet ﷺ said:

أَغْنُوهُمْ فِي هَذَا الْيَوْمِ.

Free the poor (from having to beg) on this day.[1]

Q.142. Can *ṣadaqa al-fiṭr* be given to relations?

A: Yes, relations such as siblings, uncles and aunties can be given *ṣadaqa al-fiṭr*, but one's children, parents and grandparents cannot. A husband cannot give *ṣadaqa al-fiṭr* to his wife, nor can a wife give *ṣadaqa al-fiṭr* to her husband.

Q.143. What amount has been fixed by the Shariah for *ṣadaqa al-fiṭr*?

A: *Ṣadaqa al-fiṭr* is equivalent to half a *ṣāʿ* of wheat or wheat flour, or one *ṣāʿ* of barley or barley flour. It is better to give the equivalent amount as *ṣadaqa al-fiṭr* because that will be more beneficial for the needy. *Ṣadaqa al-fiṭr* can be collectively given to one poor person.

Q.144. Does everyone pay the same amount for *ṣadaqa al-fiṭr* or is it according to one's ability?

A: *Ṣadaqa al-fiṭr* is to be paid according to one's ability. The Holy Prophet ﷺ has permitted different types of charity of *ṣadaqa al-fiṭr*. Abū Saʿīd al-Khudrī narrates:

> During the Prophetic era we used to give one *ṣāʿ* of grain as *ṣadaqa al-fiṭr* or one *ṣāʿ* of either

[1] Narrated by al-Dārquṭnī in *al-Sunan*, 2:152 §67.

> dates, barley or raisins. Wheat flour was introduced in the time of Muʿāwiya and it was comparatively more expensive, so half a *ṣāʿ* of wheat was declared to be equal to four kilos of these things.[1]

Abū Saʿīd al-Khudrī narrates in another narration:

> During the Prophetic era, we used to pay one *ṣāʿ* of grain as *ṣadaqa*. Our grains used to consist of oats, raisins, cheese and dates.[2]

Therefore, sections of society with varying ranges of income can give *ṣadaqa al-fiṭr* according to their income and financial status of the equivalent of the value of 2 kilos of wheat to 4 kilos of raisins, so that it can be the maximum benefit to the poor and needy.

Q.145. What were the reasons for setting up Minhaj Welfare Foundation? What is the role of Minhaj-ul-Quran International in the practical implementation of zakah?

A: The founding leader of Minhaj-ul-Quran International (MQI), Shaykh-ul-Islam Dr. Muhammad Tahir-ul-Qadri laid the foundations of Minhaj Welfare Foundation (MWF) on 17th October 1989. It was founded for the welfare and prosperity of those down trodden in society in order to provide them help and support in every field of life within Pakistan and throughout the world.

The Minhaj Welfare Foundation is an international welfare organisation that endeavours to help the poor and needy to live a healthy life by joining together with the affluent segment of society through mutual cooperation, brotherhood and respect. The Minhaj Welfare Foundation

[1] Narrated by al-Bukhārī in *al-Ṣaḥīḥ*, 2:548 §1437.
[2] Ibid., 2:548 §1439.

is also working in the fields of education, health and welfare. The purposes for it being set up are given below:

1. The promotion of quality education at an affordable price.
2. Grants for poor and deserving students.
3. Availability of quality and low cost medical aid for those lacking basic health needs.
4. Providing first aid, blood and ambulance services for those involved in accidents and emergencies.
5. Initiating projects to safeguard the rights and prosperity of women and children.
6. Sponsorship, education and training of orphan and needy children.
7. Assistance and relief of those affected by natural disasters.
8. Practical struggle for raising awareness of fundamental human rights.
9. Financial aid for the needy from the *bayt al-māl*.
10. Providing clean drinking water to underdeveloped areas.
11. Providing support to newly married couples by providing basic furniture, utensils and other required things for a new home alongside providing grants for the expenses of the marriage.
12. Welfare projects for the expatriate Pakistani community.
13. The moral and legal assistance of individuals through the Minhaj Reconciliation Council.
14. The setting up of education and social centres for the education, training and social support of individuals living abroad.
15. The immediate assistance of those affected by emergencies.

Q.146. WHAT ARE THE TARGETS OF THE MINHAJ WELFARE FOUNDATION?

A: The fundamental targets of the Minhaj Welfare Foundation (MWF) are given below:

EDUCATION

1. Literacy centres and primary schools.
2. One thousand high schools, Islamic centres and colleges.
3. International chartered university.
4. Setting up a university in every province in Pakistan.
5. Providing education and grants for poor and needy students.

HEALTH

1. Free medical dispensaries in every union council.
2. Arranging monthly free and low cost medical camps in every union council.
3. Minhaj Ambulance Service in all major cities and in five hundred (500) district subdivisions (*tehsil*).
4. Minhaj Hospital at the district subdivision level (*tehsil*).
5. Blood donation society across the country.

WELFARE

1. The Aghosh Care Home for five hundred (500) orphans or needy children at the central level. This project is running successfully.
2. Bait-ul-Zahra, a project to provide accommodation for four hundred (400) needy and intelligent female students. This project is in its final stages of implementation.

3. Set up branches of Aghosh in all major cities for the sponsorship, education and training of orphan and needy children.
4. Installation of water pumps in areas where water is scarce.
5. Relief efforts and emergency supplies to areas affected by natural disasters, earthquakes, flood and terrorism.
6. Provide employment through Minhaj Employment Scheme in order to tackle poverty and unemployment.

Q.147. What changes in society does the Minhaj Welfare Foundation want to bring through the system of zakah?

A: The Minhaj Welfare Foundation (MWF) wishes to work on education, health and welfare projects through the use of the zakah system and assistance of the wealthy, with the aim of not only to make a positive change in society but also to help the down trodden and destitute individuals across the world.

Allah ﷻ and the Holy Prophet ﷺ have provided guidance in order to put an end to the inequalities in society through zakah. If zakah is given from lawful earnings, that income is blessed and it multiplies in quantity. The Minhaj Welfare Foundation (MWF) wants to take society permanently out of poverty through the zakah system in the form of the *bayt al-māl* because Islam instructs the affluent members of society to help the needy and unemployed segments of society through zakah.

Minhaj Welfare Foundation (MWF) is working in the following fields:

I. EDUCATION

It is a special blessing of Allah ﷻ that under the Minhaj Welfare Foundation (MWF) in the 630 schools and eight colleges there are approximately 150,000 students from the poor and middle classes backgrounds. In these institutes thousands are studying for free. Educational grants have been awarded to bright and intelligent deserving students who come from impoverished backgrounds.

II. HEALTH

i. ANNUAL FREE EYE CAMP SURGERY CAMPS

Every year the Minhaj Welfare Foundation (MWF) arranges free eye surgery camps in different cities and especially in rural areas where along with free eye surgery, free medicine is also provided.

ii. BLOOD DONATION SOCIETIES

Minhaj Welfare Foundation (MWF) has set up blood donation societies at the national level which have thousands of men and women especially students registered who donate blood when required.

III. WELFARE

i. COLLECTIVE WELFARE

Every year Minhaj Welfare Foundation (MWF) pays for the expenditure of over a hundred poor or orphan females. How shocking it is that in this society the noble duty of marrying off daughters has also become a burden upon parents. The curse of the dowry is upsetting for the poor. In order to lift this burden from parents Minhaj Welfare Foundation (MWF) has paid for over 725 weddings in this way. The services of MWF are offered to all people without any discrimination. This is why collective weddings are also arranged for members of other religions which is a unique feature of MQI and MWF.

ii. NATURAL DISASTER RELIEF

Minhaj Welfare Foundation (MWF) is always at the forefront of relief efforts for those affected by natural disasters such floods, earthquakes, famines etc. Food, clothing, accommodation, medicines and other vital items are provided without any discrimination of creed or colour.

iii. COLLECTIVE SACRIFICE

Minhaj Welfare Foundation (MWF) follows this Abrahamic tradition and arranges collective sacrifices around the wold resulting in the meat being distributed to hundreds of thousands of families. Now this is also carried outside of Pakistan such as in Africa and Asia where meat is distributed to the poor.

iv. ᶜĪd GIFTS

The Minhaj Welfare Foundation (MWF) distributes free *ᶜĪd* packages among the poor that include flour, butter, rice, sugar and those foods specifically used in *Ramaḍān*. MWF also celebrates *ᶜĪd* with needy women and children and offers them gifts which include clothes, henna and toys for children.

v. AGHOSH

The largest project running under Minhaj Welfare Foundation (MWF) is the institution of Aghosh that caters for five hundred (500) orphans and needy children. This five story building equipped with all modern facilities has been completed. It opened up in the academic year 2012. The Aghosh grammar school is striving to promote education and awareness. Education and accommodation is provided for orphan and needy children in Aghosh by MWF. Sponsorship of a single child is inclusive of accommodation, food, clothing, educational and recreational activities.

vi. BAIT-UL-ZAHRA

Similarly the Bait-ul-Zahra project is for gifted and talented female students. Its basic structure is complete and it includes four stories including the basement. Furthermore, there are fifty-five (55) other education and welfare projects that are currently being built in Pakistan.

Conclusion

It is clear from the content of this book that the Islamic system of zakah is unique in history. No one else ever thought about such concepts nor did any other religion implement such a detailed system. Zakah fulfils the economic needs of the poor and needy and it takes effective action against the centralisation of wealth. This is a collective system because it reduces the gap between the rich and the poor, and exploitation and oppression is put to an end. Its political aspect is that at the state level it is collected and distributed through a proper system. Its moral aspect is that it purifies the wealth and heart of the donor and it is a means of creating love and brotherhood among individuals in society. In conclusion, the Islamic system of zakah is a complete, detailed and practical system which has long lasting effects upon every aspect of social life.

Bibliography

The Holy Qurʾān.

TAFSĪR

Baghawī, Abū Muhammad Ḥusayn b. Masʿūd b. Muḥammad al-Farrāʾ al- (436–516 AH), *Maʿālim al-Tanzīl*, Beirut, Lebanon: Dār al-Maʿrifa, 1407/1987.

Ibn Ḥibbān, Abū Ḥātim Muhammad b. Ḥibbān b. Aḥmad b. Ḥibbān (270–354/884–965), *al-Ṣaḥīḥ*, Beirut, Lebanon: Muʾassisa al-Risāla, 1414/1993.

Ibn Khuzayma, Abū Bakr Muhammad b. Ishaq b. Khuzayma Sulamī Nīshāpūrī (223–311/838–924), *al-Ṣaḥīḥ*, Beirut, Lebanon: al-Maktab al-Islāmī, 1390/1970.

Muqrī, Makkī b. Abī Ṭālib al- (b. 437), *Tafsīr al-hidāya ilā bulūgh al-nihāya*, Sharjah, United Arab Emirates: Kulliya al-Dirāsāt al-ʿUlyā wa al-Baḥth al-ʿIlmī, 1429/2008.

Qurṭubī, Abū ʿAbd Allāh Muhammad b. Aḥmad b. Muhammad b. Yaḥyā b. Mufarrij al-Ummawī al- (b. 671), *al-Jāmiʿ li aḥkām al-Qurʾān*, Beirut, Lebanon: Dār Iḥyāʾ al-Turāth al-ʿArabī, 1405 AH.

Ṭabarī, Abū Jaʿfar Muhammad b. Jarīr b. Yazīd b. Khālid al- (224–310/839–923), *Jāmiʿ al-bayān fī tafsīr al-Qurʾān*, Beirut, Lebanon: Dār al-Fikr, 1405 AH.

Thaʿlabī, Abū Isḥāq Aḥmad b. Muhammad b. Ibrāhīm al- (b. 427 AH), *al-Kashf wa al-bayān*, Beirut, Lebanon: Dār Iḥyāʾ al-Turāth al-ʿArabī, 1422/2002.

Hadith

ʿAbd b. Ḥumayd, Abū Muhammad ʿAbd b. Ḥumayd b. Naṣr al-Kissi (1408/1988), *al-Musnad*, Cairo, Egypt: Dār al-Fikr, 1408/1988.

Aḥmad b. Ḥanbal, Abū ʿAbd Allāh b. Muhammad (164–241/780–855), *al-Musnad,* Beirut, Lebanon: al-Maktab al-Islāmī, 1398/1978.

Abū ʿAwāna, Yaʿqūb b. Isḥāq b. Ibrāhīm b. Zayd Nīshāpūrī (230–316/845–928), *al-Musnad*, Beirut, Lebanon: Dār al-Maʿrifa, 1998 CE.

Bayhaqī, Abū Bakr Aḥmad b. al-Ḥusayn b. ʿAlī b. ʿAbd Allāh b. Mūsā al- (384–458/994–1066), *al-Sunan al-kubrā*, Beirut, Lebanon: Dār al-Kutub al-ʿIlmiyya, 1424/2003.

—. *Shuʿab al-īmān*, Beirut, Lebanon: Dār al-Kutub al-ʿIlmiyya, 1410/1990.

Bukhārī, Abū ʿAbd Allāh Muhammad b. Ismāʿīl b. Ibrahīm b. Mughīra al- (194–256/810–870), *al-Adab al-mufrad*, Beirut, Lebanon: Dār al-Bashāʾir al-Islāmiyya, 1409/1989.

—. *al-Ṣaḥīḥ*, Beirut, Lebanon: Dār Ibn Kathīr, 1414/1993.

Abū Dāwūd, Sulaymān b. Ashʿath b. Isḥāq b. Bashīr al-Sijistānī (202–275/817–889), *al-Sunan*, Beirut, Lebanon: Dār al-Fikr, 1414/1994.

Daylamī, Abū Shujāʿ Shayrawayh b. Shaharzād b. Shayrawayh al-Daylamī al-Hamdhānī al- (445–509/1053–1115), *al-Firdaws bi maʾthūr al-khiṭāb*, Beirut, Lebanon: Dār al-Kutub al-ʿIlmiyya, 1406/1986.

Ḥākim, Abū ʿAbd Allāh Muhammad b. ʿAbd Allāh b. Muhammad al- (321–405/933–1014), *al-Mustadrak ʿalā al-ṣaḥīḥ*, Beirut, Lebanon: Dār al-Kutub al-ʿIlmiyya, 1411/1990.

Haythamī, Nūr al-Dīn Abū al-Ḥasan ʿAlī b. Abī Bakr b. Sulaymān al- (735–807/1335–1405), *Majmaʿ al-zawāʾid*, Cairo, Egypt: Dār al-Riyān li al-Turāth 1407/1987.

Hindī, Ḥisām al-Dīn ʿAlāʾ al-Dīn ʿAlī Muttaqī (b. 975 AH), *Kanz al-ʿUmmāl fī Sunan al-aqwāl wa al-afʿāl*, Beirut, Lebanon: Muʾassisa al-Risāla, 1399/1979.

Kinānī, Aḥmad b. Abī Bakr b. Ismāʿīl al- (762–840 AH), *Miṣbāḥ al-zujāja fi zawāʾid*, Beirut, Lebanon: Dār al-ʿArabiyya, 1403 AH.

Ibn Mājah, Abū ʿAbd Allāh Muhammad b. Yazīd al-Qazwīnī (209–273/824–887), *al-Sunan*, Beirut, Lebanon: Dār al-Kutub al-ʿIlmiyya, 1419/1998.

Mālik, Ibn Anas b. Mālik b. Abī ʿĀmir b. ʿAmr b. Ḥārith al-Aṣbaḥī (93–179/712–795), *al-Muwaṭṭaʾ*, Beirut, Lebanon: Dār Iḥyāʾ al-Turāth al-ʿArabī, 1406/1985.

Maqdasī, Abū ʿAbd Allāh Muhammad b. ʿAbd al-Wāḥid b. Aḥmad al-Ḥanbalī al- (569–643/1173–1245), *al-Aḥādīth al-mukhtāra*, Mecca, Saudi Arabia: Maktaba al-Nahḍa al-Ḥadīthiyya, 1410/1990.

Ibn Mubārak, Abū ʿAbd al-Raḥmān ʿAbd Allah b. Wāḍiḥ Marwazī (118–181/736–798), *Kitāb al-jihād*, Lebanon: Dār Tūnīsiyya, n.d.

Mundhirī, Abū Muhammad ʿAbd al-Aẓīm b. ʿAbd al-Qawī b. ʿAbd Allāh b. Salama b. Saʿd al- (581–656/1185–1258), *al-Targhīb wa al-tarhīb*, Beirut, Lebanon: Dār al-Kutub al-ʿIlmiyya, 1417 AH.

Nasāʾī, Abū ʿAbd al-Raḥmān Aḥmad b. Shuʿayb al- (215–303/830–915), *al-Sunan*, Beirut, Lebanon: Dār al-Kutub al-ʿIlmiyya, 1416/1995.

Nawawī, Abū Zakariyyā Yaḥyā b. Sharaf b. Murrī b. al-Ḥasan b. al-Ḥusayn b. Muhammad b. Jumuʿa b. Ḥizām al- (631–677/1233–1278), *Sharḥ Ṣaḥīḥ Muslim*, Karachi, Pakistan: Qādīmī Kutub Khāna, 1375/1956.

Ibn Rāhawayh, Abū Ya'qūb Isḥāq b. Ibrāhīm b. Mikhlad b. Ibrāhīm b. 'Abd Allah (161–237/778–851), *al-Musnad,* Medina, Saudi Arabia: Maktaba al-Īmān, 1412/1991.

Shaybānī, Abū Bakr Aḥmad b. 'Amr b. Ḍaḥḥāk b. Mikhlad (206–287/822–900), *al-Āḥād wa al-mathānī,* Riyadh, Saudi Arabia: Dār al-Rāya, 1411/1991.

Ṭabarānī, Abū al-Qāsim Sulaymān b. Aḥmad b. Ayyūb b. Maṭīr al-Lakhmī al- (260–360/873–971), *al-Mu'jam al-Ṣaghīr,* Beirut, Lebanon: al-Maktab al-Islāmī, 1405/1985.

—. *al-Mu'jam al-kabīr,* Beirut, Lebanon: Dār Iḥyā' al-Turāth al-'Arabī, 1405/1985.

Ṭayālisī, Abū Dāwūd Sulaymān b. Dāwūd al-Jārūd al- (133–204/751–819), *al-Musnad,* Beirut, Lebanon: Dār al-Ma'rifa.

Tirmidhī, Abū 'Īsā Muhammad b. 'Īsā b. Sūra b. Mūsā b. Ḍaḥḥāk Salmā al- (210–279/825–892), *al-Jāmi' al-Ṣaḥīḥ,* Beirut, Lebanon: Dār al-Gharb al-Islāmī, 1998 CE.

Abū Ya'lā, Aḥmad b. 'Alī b. Mathnā b. Yaḥyā b. 'Īsā b. al-Hilāl al-Mūṣilī al-Tamīmī (210–307/825–919), *al-Musnad,* Damascus, Syria: Dār al-Ma'mūn li al-Turāth, 1404/1984.

FIQH

Ḥaṣkafī, Muhammad 'Alā' al-Dīn b. 'Alī al- (d. 1088/1677), *al-Durr al-mukhtār fī sharḥ tanwīr al-abṣār*, Karachi, Pakistan: H. M. Sa'īd Co. n.d.

Ibn al-Hammām, Kamāl al-Dīn Muhammad b. 'Abd al-Wāḥid (790–861), *Fatḥ al-qadīr sharḥ al-Hidāya*, Beirut, Lebanon: Dār al-Fikr, n.d.

Jazīrī, ʿAbd al-Raḥmān al-, *al-Fiqh ʿalā al-madhāhib al-arbiʿa*, Beirut, Lebanon: Dār Iḥyāʾ al-Turāth al-ʿArabī, n.d.

Kāsānī, ʿAlāʾ al-Dīn al- (d. 587 AH), *Badāʾiʿ al-ṣanāʾiʿ*, Karachi, Pakistan: H. M. Said Compnay, n.d.

Ibn Kathīr, Abū al-Fidāʾ Ismāʿīl b. ʿUmar (701–774/1301–1373), *al-Bidāya wa al-nihāya,* Beirut, Lebanon: Dār al-Fikr, 1419/1998.

Shawkānī, Muhammad b. ʿAlī b. Muhammad al- (d. 1173–1250/1760–1834), *Nayl al-awṭār sharḥ muntaqā al-akhbār*, Beirut, Lebanon: Dār al-Jīl, 1973 CE.

Abū Yūsuf, Yaʿqūb b. Ibrāhīm al- (113–182 AH), *Kitāb al-khirāj*, Beirut, Lebanon: Dār al-Maʿrifa, n.d.

SĪRA

Ḥalabī, ʿAlī b. Burhān al-Dīn al- (975/1044 AH), *al-Sīra al-Ḥalabiyya*, Beirut, Lebanon: Dār al-Maʿrifa, 1400 CE.

Ibn Qayyim al-Jawziyya, Abū ʿAbd Allāh Muhammad b. Abī Bakr Ayyūb (691–751/1292–1350), *Zād al-maʿād fī hudā Khayr al-ʿibād*, Beirut, Lebanon: Muʾassisa al-Risāla, 1407/1986.

HISTORY

Ibn ʿAsākir, Abū al-Qāsim ʿAlī b. al-Ḥasan b. Hibbat Allāh b. ʿAbd Allāh b. Ḥusayn al-Dimashqī al-Shāfiʿī (499-571/1105-1176), *Tārīkh Dimashq al-kabīr* (*Tārīkh Ibn ʿAsākir*), Beirut, Lebanon: Dār al-Fikr, 1995 CE.

—. *Tahdhīb tārīkh Dimashq al-kabīr,* Beirut, Lebanon: Dār Iḥyāʾ al-Turāth al-ʿArabī, 1421/2001.

Biographies

Ibn Jawzī, Abū al-Faraj ʿAbd al-Raḥmān b. ʿAlī b. Muhammad b. ʿAlī b. ʿUbayd Allāh (510-579/1116-1201), *Manāqib Amīr al-Muʾminīn ʿUmar b. al-Khaṭṭāb*, Beirut, Lebanon: Dār al-Ḥaḍāra al-ʿArabiyya, n.d.

Dictionaries

Ibn Manẓūr, Muhammad b. Mukkaram b. ʿAlī b. Aḥmad b. Abī Qāsim b. Ḥaqba al-Ifrīqī (630-711/1232-1311), *Lisān al-ʿArab*, Beirut, Lebanon: Dār Ṣādir, n.d.

Rāghib al-Aṣfahānī, Abū Qāsim Ḥusayn b. Muhammad (b. 502/1108), *al-Mufradāt fī gharīb al-Qurʾān*, Karachi, Pakistan: Kārkhāna Tijāra Kutub, n.d.